ADVANCED PRAISE FOR AMBASSADORS OF HOPE

Don't just read Donna's book. It's actually a blueprint for you to attract people into your life just the way Donna did. I'm proud of her accomplishments and even more excited about how this book has the potential to change your lifestyle for a lifetime.

Andrew Morrison

President, Small Business Camp

This book is a compilation of inspiring stories that demonstrate how being empathetic to the needs of others through volunteerism can enrich your life. I strongly recommend this book to those looking to improve their life and the lives of others.

Ellen Bambrick

Licensed Clinical Social Worker

This book is full of rich and riveting true stories. Transformation is evident in each, reminding us that human greatness is all around us and within us. Once you read this book, you're likely to find yourself feeling more alive and willing to do something to be more actively engaged in your community.

Dr. Gina Marino

Center for the Alignment of Body, Mind and Spirit

∼

All too often the literature we read is dominated by the misadventures of various rogues, urchins, ne'er-do-wells and other assorted misanthropes. How refreshing to open Donna Cariello's Ambassadors of HOPE *and savor the kindly acts and gentle spirit of life's "salt of the Earth"—the volunteers whose works of charity and generosity inspire us to do the same. Bravo, Donna Cariello—and bravo to the angels you've presented to us.*

Kieran Larkin

Theology Teacher and the author of *Messengers of God: A Survey of Old Testament Prophets*

∼

Ambassadors of HOPE *is a true feel good read! We live in a disconnected world today with all sorts of ups, downs and everything in-between. Sometimes, it's hard to feel the positives with so many negatives. What I knew for sure while reading this gold nugget is that THIS IS LIFE! As we go through the darkest times in our lives, it's knowing we are not alone and there is only one way up. This is exactly what Donna Cariello's book shows us. It doesn't matter what challenges come our way, we all have the power inside of us to choose.*

We can step up to the plate, be a role model for others and pay it forward with our actions. We all have the power to have an impact on the rest of the world. When we step outside of ourselves to he of service to the people around us, we can make magic happen. Thank you Donna for compiling so many examples of people who make a difference in the world and truly shine!

Susan Capurso

A Legacy Doula and the author of *Remember Me~The Story of My Life*

Ambassadors of HOPE *brings a different, refreshing take on the people who have made a difference in the lives of others. Inspiring real-life stories of heartache, triumph, failure, success and everything in between gives the reader a sense of purpose and a drive to want to get involved. Written in everyday words, with engaging pointed questions aimed at getting the reader thinking after each story and give the reader an almost compelling call to action.*

Peter Spanos

Business Owner, Tavolo Kitchen & Pizza

I want to thank Donna for all she does. She too has made a difference on Long Island. Hope is good . . . be positive and good things will happen!

Charles Evdos

Executive Director of Rise Life Services

AMBASSADORS OF HOPE

Help One Person Every Day

27 Inspiring Stories That Will Spark Your Desire To Make A Difference

Cover Artwork ~ Finger Painting by my son Christopher Cariello, 2006

Cover layout and design by Francis Bonnet

Photos in the word HOPE

H ~ My good friend Lhea Scotto

O ~ My nephew Jason Farrell and his son Caiden

P ~ My great nephew Connor DeLucia

E ~ My good friends Sheila & Glenn Cummins

Back cover photo of my brothers Billy and John

The torch seen in the cover photo's was a toy that my precious golden retriever Jenna aka My Jennagirl loved, she will always light up our hearts.

Sunrise 10/21/2004 ~ Sunset 4/9/2019

To

Cara

This book is dedicated to my *"FAMILY."*

*I hope that the fruits of these stories will continue to bring joy and
influence to our lives and the lives of the people we connect with
every day.*

We are on
this track together.
Pray, Play +
Never Give up Hope.

🙂

Love
Donna Cervelo

ACKNOWLEDGMENTS

This book is more than seven years in the making, and there's no way to capture every family member, friend, and team member who contributed to this endeavor in some way.

So, to all those whose names are too many to mention, thank you for helping us to make a difference one day at a time.

Special thanks to those who were hands-on in making this book possible:

The contributors of the 27 stories in this book, for their dedication to reaching out to make a difference and helping others do the same.

Special Shout-out to our editors, creative and design team: Karen Bonnet, Francis Bonnet, Lindsey Von Elm, Stephanie Larkin, Fran Monaco, Lhea Scotto, Carol Teta, and Teresa Velardi.

Thanks to Michael Mancuso for bringing the "Fired UP " song to life.

To All The Long Island Way Business and Nonprofit Contributors.

Special Shout out to my community partners who believed in my vision and made it a part of their mission. I could not have executed the plan without their dedication and support.

Amy Amato, Donna Anselmo, Angela Anton, Susan Avelli, Mickey B, Rick Bange, Rich Barbaria, Glen Boehmer, Valerie Bouris, Frank Bravata, Noreen Brittenham, Scott Brown, Waldo Cabrera, Laura Callan, Marie Cantone, Chris Catalano, Lionel Chitty, Ellen Cleary, Jeff Cohen, Rachel Coucoulas, Wendy Doerzbacher, Patricia D'Accolti, Lindsay Doyle, Tom Doyle, Donna Drake, Charles Evdos, Doreen Firestone, Beverly Fortune, Rose Fuger, Mark Gatien, Karen Garvey, Bennett Gold, Kerry Gillick-Goldberg, Barbara Ann Grova, Doreen Guma, Lloyd Gutin, David Gussin, Matthew Hall, Patrick Hanning, Mary Hauptman, Maryann Hennessey, Linda Herskowitz, John Hill, Maryann Holloway, Valentina Janek, Roger Kahn, Patricia Kunder, Karen Kutilek, Gerry Laytin, Mark Laytin, James Leveille, Patti Locurcio, Dr. Gina Marino, Jacqueline McDermott, Susan McDonald, Beth Meixner, Dean Mercado, David Miller, Donna Mis, Jed Morey, Kerry Pavan, Bob Pandolfo, Patricia Pagoaga, Maria Palagonia, Marra Parra, Debi Pisano, Patty Romano, Wayne Redman, Maria Reitano, Lucy Rosen, Jennifer Ross, Dawn Amato-Rudolph, Debbie Sardone, Patricia Schissel, Mary Scott, Mary Seifert, Heidi Shaw, Jim Skinner, Walter Skinner, Svetlana Sobel, Kurt Meyer, Matt Silva, Marvin Soskil, Peter Spanos, Kathleen Stanley, Peter Stein, Dorian Stern, Robert Sydnor, Yvonne Sydnor, Monica Tarantino, Teresa Ward, Jeffrey Weiner, David Weingarten, Robert Weitzner, Susan Winters, Helen Zagaro and Merrill Zorn.

CONTENTS

INTRODUCTION

Introduction

Everyone Has a Story

For many years, through my personal connections and my business, The Long Island Way, we have connected businesses in Long Island with nonprofits for mutual benefit. We spread awareness, raise funds, and develop strategic partnerships based on the "Spirit of Giving".

At one point, I had to step away from my business due to medical reasons. During that time, I received many emails from nonprofit organizations and met many individuals who were having serious medical and personal issues that were challenging their families. Two of them triggered me on an emotional level, sparking my desire to make a difference.

The first encounter was a phone call from my son's elementary school teacher. Her daughter was suffering from a rare disease that affected her muscles. She was a tennis player, as I was, thanks to my sister Renie who taught me how to play tennis the summer before my senior year of high school. Shortly after that, my team won Cardozo High School's Doubles Championship at the West Side Tennis Club, the venue for the Forest Hills Tennis Classic; I went on to get a tennis scholarship. I realized how fortunate I was to be healthy and able to play tennis. WHAT COULD I DO TO HELP?

The second encounter was with a woman I met at the Merrick fair who started a nonprofit organization to have medical heart testing done on teenagers. She was compelled to do this because her son died when he was in 10th grade. Her story broke my heart, and she asked me to help her. At that moment, I felt helpless because I was struggling with my own medical issues. I threw my hands in the air and asked, "GOD… HOW DO YOU WANT ME TO HELP THESE PEOPLE?"

At that moment, I heard an inner voice tell me to teach them to do what I do, and stop doing the work for them." Then, the idea came to me to create The Long Island Way Academy. I developed a curriculum called "Certified Community Ambassador Program - CCAP," and I committed to writing a book about the people who have crossed my path and have made a difference in their communities.

This book is a compilation of real-life stories of some of the most amazing people who have touched my life and who walk the walk and talk the talk. Many of them have risen above their own challenges by making a difference in the lives of others.

My heart was open to helping others; and I believe a divine intervention propelled me to ask God, "How could I market this book?" Suddenly it came to me… "Write a song called 'Fired UP!' The "Fired UP!" song will bring enthusiasm that will "spark" a call to action towards "Doing Good… is Good".

WHY 27 STORIES?

The Number 27 – "Joy Giver"

The numerological number 27 is about philanthropy and compassion in a cooperative atmosphere. It represents kind heartedness, tolerance, intelligence, team work, and betterment of humanity.

Angel Number 27 is all about living a purpose-driven life. Our guardian angels are always there to provide us with the support and inspiration necessary to live up to our highest potential.

GETTING THE MOST OUT OF THIS BOOK

STEP UP TO THE PLATE

Our hope is to encourage people to search within and find a cause or mission that makes them want to make a difference in someone else's life or community.

LISTEN WITH YOUR HEART

Enlighten your awareness in small ways and understand your purpose in the big picture about how your life experience can inspire others when shared.

SPARK A CALL TO ACTION

By recognizing your life lessons . . . good, bad and/or indifferent . . . you will help yourself heal by lending a helping hand, giving a hug, smiling at someone who needs a smile, providing meals, visiting a lonely or sick person or just giving a listening ear. These actions could very well be a lifesaver to someone! As a result, the value of helping others will certainly spill over into your own life.

BE A ROLE MODEL

Harness values that pave the way. Lead By Example. Talk the talk and walk the walk. Actions speak louder than words. Our belief theory is if they can do it, so can I, so always remember we are in this together.

PAY IT FORWARD

Think about volunteering! Your dedication, time, talents, money, and resources are instrumental to an organization, cause, or mission. The rewards are priceless and gifts unlimited when your involvement is based on your hope to impact others positively.

THESE STORIES WILL SPARK YOUR DESIRE TO MAKE A DIFFERENCE!

SECTION I

To Serve with
Love, Hope and Encouragement

Chapter One

THE PATH OF A VOLUNTEER

Karen Bonnet

"We ourselves feel that what we are doing is just a drop in the ocean. But the ocean would be less because of that missing drop."
Mother Teresa

*a*t the tender age of ten, Karen Bonnet's volunteer experiences began when she helped an infant cousin who was born severely mentally challenged. She became involved with sensory-motor "patterning"–a program of mobility exercises that aids in creeping and crawling, visual-motor training, and sensory stimulation. That experience was the beginning of her lifelong journey of volunteerism.

While raising her own children, Karen became involved in the PTA, taking on positions of leadership as well as chairing various committees. She was awarded the PTA Lifetime Membership Award for *"Outstanding Volunteer Efforts to Advocate for Children in the Oceanside School District."* As she became aware of other opportunities to enrich children's lives, Karen stepped up again. She volunteered to be a Girl Scout Leader where she served for four years, and a Den Mother for the Cub Scouts where she served for two years. During her tenure with the Girl Scouts, she met a family in Oceanside with a mentally-challenged six-year-old daughter who needed sensory-motor patterning—once again utilizing the skills she learned as a child. She immediately reached out to help the family with patterning services to improve the child's mobility.

Karen's life took on new meaning when she became active in her children's religious education program, serving as a Catechist at St. Christopher's Church, and later at St. Anthony's Church—two very rewarding experiences for her and the children she taught.

Through the years, volunteering continued to be an important part of Karen's world. She volunteered her time and talents in many other local community outreach programs. While juggling family life, a part-time job and the demands of raising children, Karen *always* actively participated in life and *always* looked at the glass as half-full.

In 2008 I had the privilege of meeting Karen through Ronald McDonald House of Long Island where she served as a public rela-

> Karen's message and goal is simple—*PAY IT FORWARD!*

tions and marketing manager. We had an immediate connection, and Karen would always welcome me with open arms. She is a genuinely real, kind and loving person to everyone she meets. Karen not only talks the talk—she walks the walk as an ambassador to those organizations she serves. Karen is a role-model whose qualities exemplify a natural-born leader and volunteer.

Today, Karen's volunteer capabilities have taken her on a new path of understanding and experience. She was a volunteer moderator and camera crewperson for a local-access television production. The show featured writers and authors from all walks of life sharing their unique experiences and stories.

Karen is the author of a children's fiction novel, *Whale Island and the Mysterious Bones*, an exciting adventure story for children, ages eight through eleven. The book takes young readers on an unforgettable journey and is packed with action and suspense.

Inspired by a documentary about starving children in Africa, Karen was so touched by the story's message it instantly sparked a call to action for her. Karen now donates a percentage of each of her book sales to *The Interfaith Nutrition Network* (*The INN*), an outstanding nonprofit organization located in Hempstead, which provides food and shelter for the needy and those undergoing a family crisis.

Karen's philosophy and attitude mirrors that of Nobel Peace Prize winner, Mother Teresa. Karen believes that giving in small ways can lift someone up and brighten that person's day.

WORDS OF WISDOM

Karen's message and goal is simple—*pay it forward*. She recommends this to us as it not only inspires us to help others in our communities and beyond—it contributes to our own personal growth as well. Help someone in need *every day*—no matter what the size of the gift—a hug, a smile, a meal, an outing, a visit, or just listening to what that person has to say. If we make it a priority to assist others in small ways, the world will be a much happier place.

QUESTIONS TO PONDER

- *Are you choosing a path as a volunteer?*
- *Do you remember a situation that helped mold you?*
- *Did you answer the call to help someone in need?*
- *Who do you want to contribute to?*

CONNECT WITH KAREN

Email: kbonnet7@gmail.com

Website: www.whaleislandstories.com

Chapter Two

BELIEVE IN YOUR COMMUNITY

Teresa Ward

"It is my belief that unless and until each of us makes the effort to improve our own community, we will never truly achieve success, personally or professionally."

eresa's family has always been extremely important to her. She grew up in a family-owned business, and that experience heavily impacted the way she chose to live her life. Her initial goal for *Teresa's Family Cleaning* was to help support her family–however, after losing her sister to cancer in 2003, her perspective changed. She started to wonder if the goals she could achieve through business could reach beyond the monetary and into the community-at-large. By that point in her career, Teresa had grown her business to employ a large staff, and had made numerous contacts across the United States. She began to involve herself socially and professionally in both national and international organizations.

Teresa's involvement with those organizations was based on the hope to raise the bar on standards and practices within the industry–and that dove-tailed well with her passion for cleaning. When she began thinking about more social and community-driven goals, Teresa realized her business had a greater purpose. By utilizing the infrastructure she had developed through her business contacts and combining her own skills with those of people she had met through her company's growth, Teresa was able to create support structures for people who were in need of help and services she could provide.

Three years after her sister's passing, Teresa, together with several fellow members of the *Association of Residential Cleaning Services International*, created a nonprofit

> Teresa was an extraordinary woman who was fearless when it came to helping others.

organization that would provide free cleaning services for women who were undergoing cancer treatment. They called it *"Cleaning for a Reason."* For her, it was something she could participate in, to honor her sister's memory, as well as provide help to women in her community-at-large. Her involvement with *"Cleaning for a Reason,"* and seeing how it changed the lives of so many women, motivated her to be further involved with social causes and the business community. *"Cleaning for a Reason"* is a national organization having helped over 33,000 women, 1,200 participating maid services and $11,000,000 donated house cleanings across the United States and Canada.

Helping her community and seeing her efforts result in making people's lives a little bit easier was something that improved her own life in ways Teresa couldn't even begin to describe. She knew her actions were not only helping people directly, they were setting an example for her children, her friends, and for other members of the business community–and with luck, they would result in more people seeing the need for success on the philanthropic and personal levels. Teresa was an extraordinary woman who was fearless when it came to helping others. She was truly a pioneer of our generation. Her efforts over the years have helped nonprofit-organizations, and her legacy lives on in the business community.

After the great success of *Cleaning for a Reason*, Teresa took her community involvement a step further by creating "*Cleaning Angels USA*," a 501c3 organization that not only provides free cleanings for women undergoing cancer treatments, but also for patients, parents, and the families of patients dealing with the hardships associated with other debilitating diseases. She had been working on creating this charity for several years, and was extremely proud to see it finally coming to fruition.

Teresa's greatest hope was that her efforts would inspire people to look to the success and betterment of others as a part of their own achievement. Giving people a hand, and helping to make the lives of others more comfortable, can be one of the greatest sources of joy and pride a person can tap into; and she encouraged as many people as possible to do their best to draw from that well.

Hopefully, Teresa's example will result in more people seeing the need for success in business, charitable, philanthropic and personal endeavors.

WORDS OF WISDOM

Something Teresa always wanted people to know is this, whether they own a business, work for a company as an employee, or work at home—she herself didn't have any special skills! She was a person, like anyone else. She wasn't formally trained to do any of the things she did throughout her life. From starting a business out of her basement, to dealing with the tragedy of her sister's death, to starting a national charity– her only real skill and her greatest asset was *tenacity*–it is what allowed her to achieve more than she ever would have thought or dreamed possible. Teresa's hope was that by letting other people know she was just like them, they might look within themselves and see that they, too, could reach beyond their own success to help others.

Sadly, Teresa left this world in 2015. Her legacy and love for people lives on in the lives of those who still support her charitable heart.

QUESTIONS TO PONDER

- *Would you like to be involved in an organization that helps raise the bar on standards and practices?*
- *What talents or skills do you possess that can help someone?*
- *What actions can you take today to help your community?*
- *In what ways have you helped make someone's life more enjoyable?*

CONNECT WITH TERESA'S DAUGHTER NICOLE

Email: NicoleWard0217@icloud.com

Phone: 631-381-5010

To learn more about *Cleaning for a Reason*, go to www. cleaningforareason.org and Cleaning Angels USA at www.- cleaningangelsusa.org

Chapter Three

MAKE A COMMITMENT

Wayne Redman

"It is not the critic who counts; not the man who points out how the strong man stumbles or where the doer of deeds could have done better. The credit belongs to the man who is actually in the arena, whose face is marred by dust and sweat and blood, who strives valiantly, who errs and comes up short again and again–because there is no effort without error or shortcoming —but who knows the great enthusiasms, the great devotions, who spends himself for a worthy cause–who, at his best, knows, in the end, the triumph of high achievement, and who, at his worst, if he fails, at least he fails while daring greatly–so that his place shall never be with those cold and timid souls who knew neither victory nor defeat."
Theodore Roosevelt

*W*ayne has always believed God placed us on this earth to share with others the impact that He has on our lives, and to use the gifts and talents that He has given each of us to help others. Wayne has been a member of the United Methodist Church of Hempstead for over 27 years and is a Certified Lay Minister. He has held many leadership and servant leadership roles in his church, and it was while he served as Church School Superintendent that he was approached by a member of the congregation and asked to join the Board of Directors of the Hempstead Boys & Girls Club which operated its Teen Center out of the United Methodist Church of Hempstead. Wayne has always recognized that our youth need trust, love, guidance and support as they grow and develop and viewed the Hempstead Boys & Girls Club as an organization that supplied these crucial needs to youth, so he joined the Board of Directors. Four years later, he was elected as Board President. Two years later, when the former Executive Director decided to retire, he was again approached by a few key members of the Board about taking on that role.

He questioned how he would be able to manage the demands of his newly started financial services practice and this potential new career; but in the back of his

> His philosophy is: "You Do You . . . Be the Best You . . . and Don't Try to Do Me."

mind, the words *"God doesn't give you more than you can handle,"* kept ringing in his head, so he accepted the position, and in March 2008, became the Executive Director of the Hempstead Boys & Girls Club.

He would see young people who were struggling with their identities turning to gangs. He witnessed an increased number of youth turning to alcohol and drugs because they didn't know where to go, young people not getting the education that was there for them, and the number of "latch key" youth on the increase–and he quickly understood that something had to change. Hempstead was becoming a place where children were being shortchanged, and Wayne knew he had to work toward changing that environment. The Hempstead Boys & Girls Club would become a platform where positive change could be implemented. Their Mission Statement: *The Hempstead Boys & Girls Club mentors, protects and develops Hempstead's most valuable resources: our children, youth, young adults and families. We help them develop their self-confidence, sense of responsibility and leadership capabilities by providing a safe place, hope and caring relationships that build character.* Their slogan: *"Great Futures Start Here!"*

Wayne's personal goal is to be a resource–someone you can turn to when you need to discover lost hope and redefine your opportunities in life. He was driven to accept this job because of the guiding principles by which he lives his life. While community outreach can be rewarding as well as thankless, it always presents the never-ending challenge of making a difference in the lives of others . . . and this always tests one's resolve and commitment

He has witnessed the growth and development of some young people who didn't initially feel they had a future. He watched one of his group members go through the program, work as a counselor-in-training, become a member of the staff, and then enroll in culinary school. That young man came back to speak at a networking event because he wanted to share his story and let others know that the Hempstead Boys and Girls Club really does mean something to our young people. It changes lives–it changed his! He has seen members recognize that hope and opportunity are real and that you just need a plan to help get you there. So, he continued as the Executive Director for nine years, because he believed that hope and opportunity for tomorrow should be available to all our youth.

Wayne is a community activist for positive youth development and is now a consultant for faith based organizations and small businesses.

> *Wayne believes that if we each spent more time on being the best we can each be–doing what we say we are going to do, when we say we are going to do it, instead of worrying about what the other guy didn't do–we would all be better off and accomplish so much more. His philosophy is: "You Do You . . . Be the Best You . . . and Don't Try to Do Me."*

Wayne lives in the community of Baldwin, NY where he attended Parent Teacher Association meetings and was involved in community youth programs such as Baldwin *PAL* (Police Athletic League) where he coached girls' basketball for four years.

WORDS OF WISDOM

Wayne was leading a bible study group on Thursday nights and was missing or rescheduling sessions because there were other things that he felt he wanted to do. One of the participants came to him and said, *"We signed up and agreed to be part of this class—this was our commitment to you—and we expect that you commit to us and lead the sessions as scheduled."* He took this to heart and has applied it in his work and his life. Wayne commits to what he is doing and prepares for it. He gives it his best shot because that is what he is supposed to do, give it his best.

QUESTIONS TO PONDER

- *Do you have a slogan you live by?*

- *Did you ever make a commitment and not follow through?*
- *Have you witnessed any areas of opportunity for our young people?*
- *Do you have a situation in your life that has redefined you?*

CONNECT WITH WAYNE

Phone: 516-707-0155

Chapter Four

LIVE A LIFE OF GRATITUDE BY STEPPING UP TO THE PLATE

Janice Pietrowicz

"If you want something, go after it.
Chase your dreams; don't wait for them to come to you!
God will guide your way if you just let Him and you believe in Him."

s a small business owner, wife and mother of three beautiful daughters, Janice has a full life. She and her husband own the Triple L Moving LLC; and she also runs her own small home-based business, as well. To make her life even more complete, she is a volunteer for St. Jude Children's Research Hospital by organizing a neighborhood bike-a-thon on an annual basis. Also, as a dedicated volunteer at the Ridge Full Gospel Christian Church, she helps organize the "Girls of Faith" Club for young girls ages six through twelve.

Prior to owning their moving company and her home-based business, Janice and her husband operated a retail furniture store for nearly twelve years in Patchogue, NY. It was during their tenure at this store that the couple began to find ways to give back to the community, whether it was through "adopting" a child during the holidays, making donations to Toys for Tots or local churches and fire departments, or running an annual food drive on September 11th in tribute to those who lost their lives that tragic day in 2001.

"After the tragedy that hit our nation on September 11th, my husband and I knew that we had a perfect outlet to help. We started a food drive for all the volunteers at Ground Zero and collected everything from food, socks, sunscreen, water–and dog food for those amazing people with animals. We are very proud of that," recalls Janice.

The motivating factor behind Janice's decision to give back to those in need was simple—it was indeed her call to action. She has a beautiful family, a loving husband, amazing daughters, and she knows that God has given her the life he feels she deserves. She owes it to God and to herself to do what she can to be a better person and to teach her children what it means to live a life of gratitude."

When she launched her business, a health and wellness company, Janice knew she could help others help themselves. But for her to be successful, she had to show her team members how to reach success, as well. Her greatest joy comes from helping others and teaching them how to do the same. Assisting people who are facing challenges, such as getting out of debt, losing weight, or getting off of medications that are life-altering, is empowering and rewarding for both Janice and the people with whom she works. She is proud of her own children, as they also are learning to get involved, and have learned the significance of giving back and paying forward.

During the annual bike-a-thon Janice organizes for St. Jude's, her children help her coordinate the event and solicit local businesses for donations. They also run the bake sale and lemonade stand for the event, which benefits the immediate community because it allows others to experience the joy of giving back. Janice is proud of her daughters and how their experiences are helping them develop into leaders in the community, as well. She is also extremely happy to be a role-model and an inspiration to others who might need some direction in their lives.

Janice's decision to volunteer with St. Jude's Children's Research Hospital came easy to her. St. Jude's never turns away a patient, no matter what their financial position may be, which is a great relief for parents and loved ones who are going through such unimaginable emotional trauma. *If she can do something to change the life of even one child, she feels she owes it to that one child to step up to the plate and give fundraising for such a worthy organization her very best shot.* Janice points out that she has been blessed enough to have three healthy, beautiful daughters and is thankful for that. It breaks her heart to hear about families going through the terrible things that come along with childhood cancers. She can't even imagine having to deal with seeing children become sick from treatments, losing their hair or the possibility of losing their lives to a senseless disease. It's just heartbreaking.

> If she can do something to change the life of even one child, she feels she owes it to that one child to step up to the plate.

WORDS OF WISDOM

Janice's advice to those who want to get involved is simple: "Don't make it about yourself —it is about others and how you can help them."

QUESTIONS TO PONDER

- *Who in your community can use your help?*
- *How can you step up to the plate today?*
- *How can you be an inspiration to your family?*
- *Are you living a life of gratitude?*
- *What gifts or talents do you have that you can use to give back?*

CONNECT WITH JANICE

Email: janlyn930@yahoo.com

Phone: 631-603-7560

ONE LITTLE VICTORY

Chris Catalano

"As a person, you are sort of defined by how you treat others that are less fortunate. Oftentimes, even those who have nothing seem to find a way to help others. If that could serve as a model to everyone, I think we'd all be in a better place."

There are many ways one can help in their community is a motto Chris Catalano believes in. Chris helps his community by giving his time and contributing funds to help a charity that is near and dear to him. He built a strong connection with the *Guide Dog Foundation* through the company he works with, *C2-It Multimedia*, where he became the Creative Director after learning about the foundation's mission. Eventually, he and his company began to regularly donate to the foundation and Chris quickly learned that there was much more to the organization than he ever realized. When the charity expressed a need for people to raise puppies, Chris knew it was time to step up and show up. That's when his involvement escalated into something bigger, and the company's participation in the Foundation grew tremendously.

Chris and his co-workers began attending classes at the *Guide Dog Foundation* and subsequently began bringing the dogs with them on various outings and, ultimately, *everywhere they went.* They learned everything they needed to know about raising/training dogs. Chris soon became a spokesperson for the charity, speaking to various groups and organizations on the merits of volunteering. During his talks he provided information, ensuring people understood how the dogs actually work and help their handlers.

On the business front, his company helped by donating time and resources to help the foundation produce a series of DVD training lessons. The most valuable skill Chris possesses is his ability to understand the big picture and how each small step or activity contributes to the overall goal. The reality is anyone can contribute and get involved on some level, no matter how small. After his initial involvement led him to realize the impact of the *Guide Dog Foundation* on so many people, he gained a sense of satisfaction in knowing that his own volunteer efforts were directly benefitting others who were facing challenges in life.

> The reality is, anyone can contribute and get involved on some level, no matter how small.

Chris was so impressed by the *Guide Dog Foundation* and the amazing ability and sensitivity of the dogs to their handlers, that he adopted one of the dogs that was released from the foundation.

This eventually led him to become involved in animal-assisted therapy with his own dog, Andi. Bringing his dog to residents in various facilities they visit brings Chris the greatest satisfaction and sense of pride; as he is able to witness the immediate, positive impact a therapy-dog has on individuals. Chris' work with animal-assisted therapy has brought his own goal to fruition, which includes providing joy and happiness to the residents of those facilities they visit, and bringing encouragement for others to join the program.

Of all his accomplishments, Chris reflects on the "little moments" as the most memorable. He describes it this way: *"When a person in an advanced state of Alzheimer's, who is not aware of their surroundings, suddenly perks up and smiles when petting your dog – it's an amazing feeling. It's just a series of one little victory after another."*

The mantra by which Chris lives each and every moment is *"Do it because it needs to be done."* Joy and fulfillment are his great rewards.

WORDS OF WISDOM

Getting involved in a charity for which you have a passion is a motivating factor in itself. Chris has always felt it was important to do something to help others, whether it was donating money or being a hands-on contributor to the cause. Once you start looking around, it's not hard to find something or someone that could benefit from your time and experience.

QUESTIONS TO PONDER

- *Who could benefit from your services? Are you a hands-on person?*
- *Do you or your company have the resources to donate your time or finances to a nonprofit organization?*

- *Are you willing to reach out to your network of community-minded people?*
- *Have you experienced one little victory?*
- *What cause speaks to your heart?*

CONNECT WITH CHRIS

Email: catalano2@yahoo.com

Phone: (631) 472-1744

Website: GuideDog.org

Chapter Six

THE GIFT OF BEING PRESENT IN THE MOMENT

Joyce Barron

"Be the best you can be in every moment—when you shine brightly by being the light, you give permission for another person to stand with you to shine, adding to the brightness."

*J*oyce Barron is inspired to always be her best. To this day, Joyce has strived to do just that. She volunteers for Smithtown Methodist Church as a member of the Board of Trustees and has used her skills/training in Dale Carnegie Human Relations to help her church and the parishioners in whatever way she can. She is a volunteer at the *Victims Information Bureau of Suffolk Family Violence and Rape Crisis Center in Hauppauge (VIBS)*, as well as an on-call volunteer for hospital emergency-room rape victims, giving them emotional support and encouragement to get counseling from *VIBS*. Joyce's full-time position as a recruiter is just another part of her life that helps to connect all the dots. Her heart, however, is in assisting in the healing of women and children who are suffering. Joyce is empowering them to be strong and to leave their abusers, so they won't have to live with shame for the rest of their lives.

"The sooner they learn there is help, the sooner they can learn how loved, loveable, and worthy they are," recalls Joyce.

Joyce was inspired to get involved first from helping at her church; later, she learned about *VIBS* because of the breakup of a personal relationship left her in a state of depression and blaming herself for the loss of the relationship. The shame and humiliation of having strong feelings for a person who showed little regard for her left her puzzled and wondering why she would tolerate this behavior.

As she reflected on her own childhood, she realized she had learned to shut down her own needs in order to feel safe in her own home. Everything was focused on not upsetting her father, and she didn't realize how unconscious she was until Joyce was in her late 40s when she finally addressed her feelings of unworthiness and shame.

"Help one person at a time and their world will change, and the people they impact will be changed too."

When Joyce became aware that her feelings stemmed from years of verbal and emotional abuse in her childhood, she vowed to help other women and children living in abusive situations, showing them that there is support available and they can feel safe and loved again. Joyce's mission is to teach women and children that they can protect themselves by having confidence and support to create healthy boundaries and good relationships in a safe environment.

Her community service efforts have not only benefitted the

community and those whose lives she's touched, it has helped her to learn more about herself. Joyce now recognizes her purpose, her strengths and her compassion. It has also humbled her and taught her how to live in the present moment, especially when helping those who are suffering abuse. Choosing a cause like *VIBS* was a natural fit for Joyce because she personally knows that people who are suffering through domestic violence, rape, verbal, and emotional abuse are reticent to talk about it as they are ashamed or embarrassed. She is very proud to be a volunteer with this organization whose mission is to help women and children know there is a way out of an unhealthy relationship to break the cycle of abuse and build love and confidence in their hearts. Joyce encourages others to search within–and find a cause that makes them want to make a difference in someone else's life.

"Help one person at a time and their world will change; and the people they impact will be changed, too."

WORDS OF WISDOM

As a source of encouragement and inspiration to others who are searching for ways to give back, Joyce advises them–*"Ask yourself if there is an issue that causes you to feel enraged or passionate; and if there was something you could do to stop it, would you? If you can discover what brings out this emotion, you will locate the organization or individuals that need your help.*

QUESTIONS TO PONDER

- *Have you ever tolerated unacceptable behavior?*

- *Do you have a life experience that you can share to help someone else?*
- *Will you write down a story from your past to share with someone else who may be going through something similar?*
- *Will you do that to help someone else today?*

CONNECT WITH JOYCE

Email: joyce.barron@ymail.com

Chapter Seven

CYCLE OF LIFE

Joanne Yetkofsky

A quote that has followed her all her life:
"To Thine Own Self Be True."

*J*oanne and her husband Bobby lived in Wantagh, a suburb of Long Island, New York for over 36 years where they raised their five children: three boys, and two girls. If only her home could talk, it would tell quite a detailed description of the situations and circumstances that led to her being a caregiver many years later to her two grandchildren by a mandated court system.

Joanne at fifty-two-years-old and Bobby at fifty-six-years-old had very different dreams of how their lives would be after children. Their mutual decision to reach out for professional help, having very close friends in their lives, and praying day and night had helped them to make a decision they felt they could live with for the rest of their lives.

Their daughter had made some bad choices in her life which lead to domestic violence. Distraught by this turn of events,

Joanne and her husband had to take affirmative action to protect their grandchildren. They became advocates and voices of reason by starting proceedings for the welfare and safety of the children. Their actions were solely based on the hope that their daughter would seize this opportunity to straighten out her own life, being able to properly care-for herself–and in due time, for her girls. The journey led to life-changing experiences in the process.

Joanne was diagnosed as clinically depressed due to fear, uncertainty, and exhaustion from this whole process. She was grateful when her friend said, *"Either God's grace is on you to do this, or it is not."* In spite of her physical and emotional emptiness, her faith and her friends (*Angels*) along the way, gave her the strength to face all her inner demons and show up, numerous times shaking, yet cradled in God's care and protection. She was facing the horrifying decision to place an order of protection and an eviction notice on her own daughter to protect her grandchildren.

Many times as she sat in the courtroom awaiting the trial, filled with nervous energy, she would glance behind the judge at the inscription on the wall that read,

> Joanne's hope is that this story will inspire readers to say, "Yes!" to God's invitation to be of service

"In God We Trust." Joanne immediately felt a sense of relief and was filled with faith and trust that God's will would be done. To this day she carries a penny with that same inscription as a reminder of her faith. Joanne believes she has been blessed to be of service to her grandchildren, who in turn have helped her grow beyond her wildest dreams.

Living the 12-step program inspired her journey, appearing futile at times. Her favorite song, *"What a Difference a Day*

Makes," has helped her deal with the physical challenges, financial fears, and emotional illness surrounding her family. As a family unit, they have continued to "pay it forward" by bearing witness to those they would help by God's power, strength, and way-of-life. Her own upbringing had taught Joanne not to trust or be vulnerable, and not to expose the truth or bring light to that truth. God's plan has always been to use these weaknesses to give birth to new hope daily, to deepen her faith, give her a purpose and a reason to be. In many ways, inspired by living the 12-step program daily and showing up authentically for herself and those who are part of her life, God has used her, a weak suffering soul, to help the healing of other like-minded people. This has been one of the greatest gifts bestowed on her, to have a purpose where she never felt she had one. How miraculous for her, to go from terrified loneliness, isolated and lost in a deep dark hole, to be given new skills and behaviors—to have a voice to speak up and out.

Joanne continues to use these tools wherever she goes to share her experience, strength, and hope. Being blessed and loved by all who interact with her childlike faith and openness to being used by God to reach out to other sick and suffering people. She surrounds herself with loving, caring, and nurturing angels who help her set goals and carry the message of peace, love, and joy.

WORDS OF WISDOM

Joanne's hope is that this story, not her personally, will inspire readers to say, "Yes!" to God's invitation to be of service, no matter how impossible it may appear. Renew your mind as an instrument in this darkness, in this evil that is upon us, and let the light illuminate His wonders performed through all who reach out to serve. Although there were many times when she wanted to quit, another reason, another spark, another opportunity arose for Joanne to be obedient to God's plan, no matter when in her own small vision, it seemed impossible. Say "YES" to the golden opportunities of serving others.

QUESTIONS TO PONDER

- *Do you give generously?*
- *Do you make decisions that you can live with?*
- *Do you take time to sit and reflect on your purpose?*
- *Important! What are your motives?*
- *Are you too busy to hear the call of God or see the light of my inner path?*
- *Are you living or existing for more? (for what)*
- *Through what weakness have you found your greatest strength?*

CONNECT WITH JOANNE

Phone: 516-735-7060

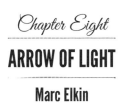

Chapter Eight

ARROW OF LIGHT

Marc Elkin

"The feeling of seeing these boys actually grasp what I have taught them is such a rewarding experience. To know that the scouts leave my meeting and are able to share what they have learned or experienced with their parents is amazing."

Scouting began in 1907 when Robert Baden-Powell, a lieutenant general in the British Army, held the first Scouting encampment on Brown Sea Island in England. Baden-Powell wrote the principles of Scouting in *Scouting for Boys* (London, 1908). In 2012, Scouting has over 38 million members worldwide and growing strong. The program to teach young boys and mold them into fine young men carries an experience that is unsurpassed.

As a dad who was in Cub Scouting himself, Marc had the rush and excitement to get his young boy to join when he turned five years old. A Tiger cub, his son, Justin joined and was on his way to reaping the benefits of scouting. Remembering the program from his own childhood experiences, he inquired through the local committee as to how he could become a Cub Scout leader. Eight years later, Marc became the Cub Master of Cub Pack 689, Seaford.

It only took him a little under a year to realize that there is a great deal more to scouting that the stereotypical scout image most people tend to think of, camping, knot tying, campfire sing-alongs, to name a few. The Core Values of Scouting are as follows: Citizenship, Compassion, Cooperation, Courage, Faith, Health and Fitness, Honesty, Perseverance, Positive Attitude, Resourcefulness, Respect, and Responsibility. These values are taught in many different ways at age-appropriate levels, showing scouts the way.

Believing in these qualities, Marc volunteered to become a Cub Scout Leader. He wanted to participate with his son as he excelled in these areas and watch him grow into a fine young man. He wanted him to have a great experience while benefitting from the program. Once Marc became his son's Cub Scout leader, it was only a matter of time until he realized how important the program was, his desire to help other boys benefit from this program came to life.

As a Den Leader, Marc had the pleasure of helping these boys harness the scout values through nature, arts and crafts, friendship bonding, writing, and drawing.

"I always try to step back and put myself at their age level, allowing myself to become a kid with them,"

Only a scout leader can vouch for how rewarding it is to see a young boy grow through the scouting program. Marc has seen his son and his buddies start out making shapes out of pipe cleaners to using power tools by the end of scouting experience they earned the highest level of Cub Scouting, the *Arrow of Light*.

Every week, Marc would plan for the next meeting. What to do . . . what to say . . . and what to teach the boys in a way they would understand at their age level. "I always try to step back and put myself at their age level (wasn't too hard to do), allowing myself to become a kid with them," says Marc. He would sit on the floor with them, or run with them in an outdoor game, or just make silly sounds and jokes, making them laugh.

The feeling of seeing these boys actually grasp what he had taught them was a highly rewarding experience for Marc. He was amazed when the scouts would leave his meeting and were able to share what they had learned or experienced with their parents. This would always inspire him to start his preparation for the next meeting. Marc was as excited as the boys were to start the next activity and head toward the path of earning their next badge.

As time lapsed on in Cub Scouting, Marc realized it was time for him to jump even higher for the boys. It was time for him to become the Pack's "Cub Master." The endless tasks to plan pack nights, making sure all the dens were doing what they should, hashing out all the problems, complaints and issues voiced by the parents, and making sure all leaders were instilling the Core values in Scouting as the program teaches was Marc's responsibility.

With the "Cub Master" thing down pretty good and all running smoothly, it became easier to take the time to stop and talk to the boys, see what's happening, what they are up to. It's almost like a school principal saying, "Hi," to a student in passing. All the plans and meetings that go well are rewarding to a Cub Master, but the biggest reward for him is when a scout takes a minute to give Marc a high five or say good bye for the night.

That inspires him to keep doing what he is doing. It's ALL for the boys—to keep the program alive, to live scouting through the scout's eyes, seeing what they see.

Marc was lucky to have his younger son in scouting, buying him more time to stay with the Pack. When his son graduated in 2014, Mark had to had to make the hardest speech ever . . . farewell to the graduating scouts and farewell to the pack. It was also his Cub Master retirement party! Ten years in the making. He has been told every year by the scouts who graduated that he would be missed.

In today's world, full of the everyday hustle and bustle of our lives: school, sports, family, home care, we tend to forget to enforce the important skills children should harness while they are growing up. Marc has always believed a child should learn self-reliance, self-confidence, discipline, and respect in order to grow up and succeed in whatever they choose to do, using these qualities to back them up.

WORDS OF WISDOM

Walking the path to the *Arrow of Light,* Marc starts to get a little sad, knowing the boys will move on and graduate from Cub Scouting to Boy Scouting. He knows they will persevere with all their experiences and skills, carrying all they learned in Cub Scouting over to their Boy Scouting adventure. As a Leader, the most rewarding experience is to know we have done our job well and the scouts are well prepared.

The Boy Scout Motto - "Be Prepared"

After his youngest son graduated from Cub Scouts, it was time for Marc to join forces with the Boy Scouts by becoming an assistant Scoutmaster. He then had the opportunity to see the light of his own experience shine together with those boys.

QUESTIONS TO PONDER

- *Where and when did you learn about core values?*
- *How do you incorporate friendship bonding in your life?*
- *When was the last time you rolled around allowing yourself to become a kid again?*
- *How have you used your own life experience to benefit others?*

CONNECT WITH MARK

Email: asmtroop689@gmail.com

Phone: (516) 816-3764

SECTION II

*Empowering Guides That
Enhance Lives*

Chapter Nine

A MEMOIR OF LOVE

Joe Satriano

"Never Give Up . . . Never Surrender!"
Susan Satriano's mantra,
from the movie *Galaxy Quest*

*J*oe Satriano, a long-time Oceanside resident, was a high school math teacher for more than thirty years. As a happy family man, he enjoyed spending time with his wife, Susan and their two sons–until their lives changed drastically: Susan discovered she had breast cancer. She battled the disease for 13 years; and Joe was there for her every step of the way, even retiring early from his job to care for her every need.

After Susan died in 2005, Joe felt lost—the void stretched on for six months. Knowing how the journey with Susan's disease affected his two boys emotionally, he discovered a way to give back. Joe began writing as a cathartic means to cope with his loss, and his writing soon blossomed into a meaningful project.

His inspirational book, *"In Sickness and in Health: A Memoir of Love,"* describes his life with Susan and their two sons, and how they handled the cancer diagnosis with *"love, laughter, and humor."*

Joe launched the *Susan Satriano Memorial Foundation* in 2006 with the proceeds from Susan's life insurance policy. In the first year, the funds were divided as scholarships among four Oceanside High School seniors who each had a parent who had suffered or was suffering with cancer. Since its inception, this nonprofit organization has grown immensely—providing 1,300 scholarships to students locally and across the country with more than $900,000 in scholarship funds making a difference in the lives of others in honor of his wife.

Joe's mission is to continue to grow the foundation–aiding these silent sufferers across the nation and watching his mission expand and touch other families' lives, as well. He is truly proud to have been able to turn around the ultimate heartbreak in his own life and reshape his existence externally, giving hope and optimism to teenagers whose plight usually goes unnoticed.

> "Life is short, and no one knows what is around life's next corner, so live it up . . . enjoy all that you have."

One of the skills Joe learned along the way took him completely by surprise. When he penned his book, he never dreamed he had the ability to write such a moving memoir, which makes the reader laugh, cry, and live his memorable moments along with him. People who have read his book tell Joe that it has inspired them to move forward in their lives through the way Susan and he dealt with the disease. Not only does the book help others to move forward–one-hundred percent of the proceeds from the book sales go to *The Susan Satriano Foundation.*

> *Joe's own philosophy is to give back in some way, anyway that one can, because "giving back is probably the most incredible thing one can offer." His passion for the foundation and its mission is not only a cathartic means of dealing with a tragedy; it is a way to lend support to others, especially teenagers (he calls them the "silent sufferers") who are dealing with the sickness or loss of a parent. He knows that if he can pick himself up after such great loss, they can too.*

WORDS OF WISDOM

"Life is short, and no one knows what is around life's next corner, so live it up . . . enjoy all that you have . . . friends, family, nature, etc. Life is our most precious commodity, so don't squander it away—enjoy each moment!"

"It is so easy to help your fellow man—it doesn't have to be monetary; it can take the form of a pat on the back, lending an ear, or just simply being there for someone in need."

QUESTIONS TO PONDER

- *Have you ever been faced with a challenge that gave you the opportunity to reflect on your life?*
- *If so, how can you turn that situation around to help others?*
- *In what ways do you show your appreciation for life?*
- *Do you take the time to give love to family and friends?*

CONNECT WITH JOE

Email: joe@susansatrianofoundation.com

Website: www.susansatrianofoundation.com

Phone: Joe Satriano 516-603-5520

Chapter Ten

TICKLE YOUR HEART

Marie Cantone

*"Go with an open heart and a willing soul.
Think about what really makes you happy and the cause you are
passionate about."*

$\mathcal{M}$arie Cantone became a volunteer because she has a special place in her heart for children, and is particularly passionate about her work with individuals with special needs, spending time with them whenever she can. This passion has led her to wear two hats in her life. When she is not working as a full-time Senior Insurance Advisor, Marie is involved as a volunteer with Camp Northstar, a nonprofit organization located in Islip, which offers programs for children and adults with developmental disabilities.

A typical day at the camp includes providing leadership and creative activities such as talent shows, arts and crafts, and yoga for kids and adults with special needs, ranging in age from ten to sixty. Marie's personal goal is ongoing advocacy for the individuals at Camp Northstar; and she spreads the word with hope, showing others the joy of giving. She also reaches out to people on social-media sites like Facebook and LinkedIn as part of her ongoing quest to generate awareness for this great cause.

Different things tug at our hearts in ways that make us want to do something. Camp Northstar is a magical place that continually makes our hearts sing. The volunteers make a big difference in the campers' lives, and more importantly, those campers make a big difference in their lives. Marie has experienced many volunteer activities and will continue to be a helping hand. She believes this is a lifelong commitment. Her own life mantra expresses how she feels:

"Change your thoughts, change your world."

Marie started volunteering in high school when she began assisting a three-year-old toddler with Down's Syndrome. This experience affected her in such a profound

> She spreads the word with hope, showing others the joy of giving.

way that it has led her to follow a lifelong course which includes advocating for individuals with special needs, nationally and internationally. That beautiful three-year-old toddler was highly instrumental in deciding Marie's path of volunteerism in the years ahead. Although she does not have a child with special needs, she explains that being of assistance and of benefit to the community and *paying it forward* is what is most important to her.

Marie's experience at Camp Northstar not only benefits the campers and the community, it has changed her own life in many positive ways. As she points out, she is overjoyed to give everyone the opportunity to learn more about themselves, gain confidence, and grow individually. When Marie asks other people when they are the happiest, many say it is when they are doing something for someone else. Volunteering is a blessing which keeps our minds from becoming self-absorbed. She emphasizes how magical individuals with different abilities are.

"So many people are hesitant when it comes to volunteering with individuals with special needs, but if they opened up their hearts and minds the rewards are incredible."

In recalling a fond memory about a timid child at one of the camp's talent shows, she thoughtfully explained, *"I saw a painfully shy child bloom at the talent show—wanting to be in the show but feeling terrified. After a lot of encouragement, she got on the stage and opened up like a butterfly . . . she was amazing!"*

Marie's love of people with special needs and her experience at Camp Northstar has led her to create *Changing Hands*, a nonprofit organization providing a unique partnership where businesses and nonprofits share a mutual benefit from the talented volunteer force of individuals of all abilities completing and orchestrating projects and events. *Changing Hands* strives to bring joy, compassion and opportunity to all its participants.

Marie's purpose and vision is to always PAY IT FORWARD.

WORDS OF WISDOM

Marie's suggestion to those who wish to be more involved in their community is: *"Go with an open heart and a willing soul.*

Think about what really makes you happy and what makes you cry. It has to be something that you are passionate about."

While Marie is humble about her many accomplishments, she challenges you to seek out ways to get involved.

QUESTIONS TO PONDER

- *What cause is tugging at your heart?*
- *How can that cause ignite you to action?*
- *How and where in your community can you pay it forward?*
- *How have your caterpillar experiences transformed you into a butterfly?*

CONNECT WITH MARIE

Email: Marie@familyfinancialservices.info

info@ourchanginghands.org

Phone: 631-433-0656

www.themedicareanswers.com/mariecantone

To learn more about *Changing Hands*, go to

www.ourchanginghands.org

To learn more about Camp Northstar, go to

www.campnorthstar.org

Chapter Eleven

THE WELL-NEEDED GRASS ROOTS

Ginny Salerno

"Helping others organize an event or volunteer for a charity is very gratifying for me. That is why I urge you to volunteer for something in your lifetime. Don't think you are only one person and you can't make much of a difference in the world. If you have a belief in your abilities, set goals, and surround yourself with other like-minded people you can change the world!"

Ginny Salerno's inspiration to do better for Long Islanders battling cancer stemmed from her personal experience participating in a three-day national breast cancer walk. She learned that the dispersement of those funds would barely make an impact for Long Islanders battling cancer. Ginny was determined to create an event that would keep the funding on Long Island for local grass-roots organizations who were providing services to those affected by cancer. Her perseverance and motivation resulted in the founding of the Long Island 2-Day Breast Cancer Walk (LI2DAY), an organization where 100% of the funds raised go back into the Long

Island community. Ginny is the Executive Director of LI2DAY, the nonprofit organization she founded 15-years ago in Hauppauge, NY.

During the years following LI2DAY's inception, the nonprofit has grown and expanded its mission in 2014 to include funding for all cancers at beneficiary organizations whose by-laws and funding permit them to do so. LI2DAY beneficiary organizations span from Manhasset to Montauk. Ginny runs into people all the time who LI2DAY has helped or someone who is battling or knows someone with breast cancer. Knowing she is making a difference for so many makes this initiative worthwhile. Together, through her diverse beneficiary organizations, they are helping people to have a fighting chance against breast cancer and all cancers.

Programs that LI2DAY funds have grown, too, and encompass multicultural, socioeconomic and age-specific populations. Programs include counseling services for

> "Never give up, don't take 'NO' for an answer, and how hard could it be?"

children affected by their parent/guardian's cancer; alternative wellness programs such as acupuncture, massage, meditation, and exercises designed for those with or recovering from cancer, as well as hospice programs that provide comfort and dignity to the patients and their families at the end-stage-of-life. LI2DAY has grown to three events—always going the extra mile to fight cancer. The roster of events include the 13.1 Mile Walk and two Hope Runs Here 5K Run/Walk events.

In 15-years LI2Day has been instrumental in raising over seven-million dollars ($7,000,000) to fund programs at local grass-roots organizations that provide support services to cancer patients and their families, educational programs, research, as well as bring awareness to the local communities. Ginny truly believes that one-hundred percent of the funds raised by participants should go to the cause, and she is proud to acknowledge that she has done just that. LI2DAY funded programs have helped assist over 171,000 Long Islanders, $238,000 in scholarships have been awarded, and $297,300 has been granted for breast cancer research here on Long Island.

As a leader, Ginny is aware that running an organization of this magnitude is simply not possible without dedicated volunteers and a collaborative effort with LI2DAY beneficiary organizations. She is gratified by the realization that she is making a difference for Long Islanders. The organization has come a long way since it first launched in 2004–continuing today with an amazing group of like-minded people. None of this would be possible without an enormous amount of work put in year-round by a small army of dedicated individuals, support from municipalities and businesses to ensure the events are successful.

> Ginny shares, *"It is integral to listen to suggestions from others and utilize suggestions that will make the event better. If you don't know how to do something, surround yourself with people who do. Volunteers are imperative to any organization–their dedication, time and talents add to the success of the mission."*

Ginny's background and life experience in Exercise Science made her the perfect candidate to organize and coordinate the LI2DAY events, which annually attract thousands of participants. Her relationships and direct involvement in marathons, triathlons, and half-marathons have given her the knowledge needed to run efficient events that includes the provision of healthy, tasty meals, plenty of beverages, post-event awards, commemorative t-shirts and much more—making the experience memorable, meaningful, and fun for all participants.

Ginny's advice: *"Never give-up, don't take 'NO' for an answer, and how hard could it be?"*

Words of Wisdom

Helping others through organizing an event or volunteering for a charity is rewarding and personally satisfying, as Ginny has learned over the years. Regarding advice to those who are searching for ways to assist their communities, Ginny suggests asking yourself how your talents might benefit other people who are less fortunate. Do some soul searching–maybe a loved one is afflicted with a disease or disability. Only then will you find a cause that is dear to your heart.

QUESTIONS TO PONDER

- *Are you unhappy about how an organization you have interest in is running?*
- *If yes, are you willing to be that person who takes the first step to make a difference?*
- *How can you use your talents to help support a nonprofit or charitable organization?*
- *Can you build a team of community-minded people?*
- *If yes, start writing a list of your team members.*

CONTACT GINNY

Ginny Salerno, Founder & Director LI2DAY

Email: info@li2daywalk.org

Website: www.li2daywalk.org

Phone: 631-863-2DAY (2329)

Chapter Twelve

LIFELINE TO SUPPORT MOTHERHOOD

Linda Lisi Juergens

"You will get all you want in life, if you help enough other people get what they want." ~ Zig Ziglar

*L*inda began her journey as a member and volunteer at the National Association of Mothers' Centers, Inc. (NAMC) now known as *Mom-mentum* at the local and national levels, eventually working part-time at the national office and ultimately serving as Executive Director from 2000 to 2013.

Her involvement began because she was looking for intellectual stimulation after she gave birth to her first child in 1977. She read about a new program for mothers, run by mothers–and it was this program that helped her break her isolation, changing her focus from work and herself, to keeping a fragile newborn alive and well.

She found friends, and more importantly, validation of the intense joys and challenges of motherhood. Mom-mentum offered her the opportunity to learn more about normal child development; a chance to be reflective about how she wanted to parent, as well as knowing when an outside assessment might be warranted. It also exposed her to many parenting theories, ideas and tips shared in a non-judgmental atmosphere. Since this was delivered mom-to-mom by volunteers, she knew she wanted to be part of the organization to allow other women coming after her to experience this life-changing and life-affirming program.

Mom-mentum has benefited the community by highlighting the dramatic changes motherhood brings into women's lives and by providing the support and tools that they need to be thoughtful and mindful in how they help their children develop and thrive. What truly makes this program unique is that it makes women realize that this support helps them to be the best mothers they can be as well as offering them an opportunity to develop themselves as women by learning to become advocates for themselves and their families. For Linda, becoming involved as a volunteer felt like the right thing to do and then paying it forward allowed others to have the same opportunity to participate.

Her mission is to reach more mothers, in more settings, with the unique Mothers' Center support program, making it clear that the work of mothering is vital and important work in society—

"Before embarking on something new, learn by asking others who've 'been there, done that' about what they learned in that process."

but it is often invisible and greatly undervalued. Mothers are chronically under-served . . . most people see them as the nurturers who provide for everyone else in their families (and often in their communities, as well), but who don't qualify for support in this critical role of *"mother."*

Linda's volunteerism has helped establish two local Mothers' Centers. She embarked on a clear and focused advocacy effort regarding the economic impact of caregiving. They partnered with a nationally renowned journalist, author and lecturer on economic issues–Ann Crittenden, author of *"The Price of Motherhood: Why the Most Important Job in the World is Still the Least Valued,"* to help inform women/mothers about the influences and circumstances outside of them that impact their ability to support themselves and their families. These include popular culture, business practices and policies, as well as public policy. She has made *Mom-mentum* well known locally on Long Island, nationally and in the international motherhood research community. You can keep pace with technology advances through their website, electronic newsletter, blogs, online programs, and social media presence.

Being involved with helping to sustain this vital mother-centric, community-building program gave Linda a personal feeling of fulfillment. The discussion and interactions became more focused on commonalities with mothers rather than their differences. The Mothers' Center program benefits communities because it creates a stronger sense of camaraderie, promotes mutual respect, improves communication and empathy, as well as provides opportunities for women to grow and develop. Participants learn interpersonal communication skills, e.g. negotiating and conflict resolution skills, which they use in discussion groups while parenting their children, in communications with their spouse or partner, at work and within the medical and educational systems. Once these skills are learned, they change the way people will act/react/behave for the rest of their lives.

Linda excels in her ability to know her style of leadership and communication skills. She has shown enormous courage to be rigorously honest and up front with all whom she encounters. Her cool demeanor and focused listening skills have enabled her to respond to adverse situations with empathy, and sound words that express a common ground–allowing "you" to be "you."

> Linda says, "Don't compare yourself to others. Stay focused on how you can reach your goals in your unique way. Before embarking on something new, learn by asking others who've 'been there, done that' about what they learned in that process–and about paying it forward by simply helping others."

Linda has experienced first hand the benefits of a mothers' development and has enhanced her chances of mothering to the best of her ability—thereby affecting the wellbeing and development of her children and the functioning of her family as a whole.

WORDS OF WISDOM

Mothers' Center has changed the direction of Linda's life and has been a lifeline for thousands of women. In our society, people assume that mothers do not need anything from others as they are the caregivers and nurturers. The first question she gets when she mentions that the organization serves mothers is whether these women are homeless, poor, drug-addicted or mentally ill. There is no question in the minds of others that the transition to motherhood for ALL mothers is a challenging and transformational time. They will never be the same again. Motherhood is complex, challenging, rewarding, frustrating, growth-promoting, exasperating, all-encompassing, 24/7 and lasts well beyond your child's 18th birthday. That is why Linda believes that all women deserve support, services, information and a community in which to mother.

QUESTIONS TO PONDER

- *Get started by listing 3 organizations you can get involved in by becoming a member or volunteer first?*
- *Before you run out to form your own charity, do careful research to make sure someone else hasn't already started something similar!*
- *When you find that organization that's not exactly doing what you envisioned, they might be interested in adding your idea to their services or collaborating with you to find ways/resources to address the need you've identified.*
- *What issues/causes/populations speak to your heart?*
- *Conversely, do you recognize a need that is not being filled?*
- *Are you willing to give your input to enhance or make changes?*

CONNECT WITH LINDA

Email: LLJWordWorks@gmail.com

Website: www.mom-mentum.org

Phone: (516)662-5798

Chapter Thirteen

HER TIME HAS COME

Madona Cole-Lacy

"The only time it is about you, is when you show basic respect towards your co-laborers as your key contribution towards achieving the goals of a common cause."

adona is a visual/teaching artist and entrepreneur whose inspiration came from several places. As a little girl born and raised in Sierra Leone, West Africa, she watched her parents address the needs of community members in many ways. As a result, she grew up expecting that outreach was a natural phenomenon of life. Her great-grandmother was extremely community-oriented as well! She grew up doing that which she witnessed as a little girl, with highly motivated and community-oriented family members as her role models.

Another big part of Madona's inspiration came from her heightened awareness of on-going self-improvement for all, and a need to share solutions to obstacles she had encountered in her adult life. These lessons and experiences came directly from her own life's journey as a teacher, a single-parent (divorcee), and one who was brought up with a strong sense of cultural identity and respect for her fellow human beings. These individuals have contributed tremendously to what has inspired her to act to empower others.

She has chosen not to restrict herself to any one member or group of people in the Long Island community where she lends a hand. She sees herself as an active, caring and legitimate member of any "village." Madona may find herself in the African village–or its American counterpart! For many years, through her art-related workshops and her wearable art business ventures, she has tailored components of her programs and products to reflect this concept. Her authentic free-spirited personality enables her to impact and inspire people wherever she goes.

Madona's quest for inspiration from meaningful occurrences in her life sparked her decision to provide free *Dignity Enhancement* workshops to women and girls

> She wants to be able to show that it is indeed alright for people to wear their hearts on their sleeves.

experiencing hair loss as a result of the effects of chemotherapy. The workshop was born of a personal experience with a friend of hers. When Madona walked into her friend's hospital room, she was devastated to see Carolyn, a beautiful, energetic, spiritually energized lady, had been attired in a blue paper bouffant. As a designer of wearable art whose aim is to provide a sense of dignity to the wearer, she felt compelled to get on with the job she did best and created a piece of headwear which she could present as a gift to her friend–one that would lend dignity to Carolyn as she lay in her hospital bed!

Shortly after, Madona responded to the need for comfortable and elegant headwear especially designed for women experiencing hair-loss. The positive response her headwear designs have received has heightened her compassion for those living with cancer and her commitment to making a difference in their lives. The ability to supply headwear and other wearable art needs of women of all shapes and sizes gives her great satisfaction and pleasure as she receives the joy and gratitude expressed by those for whom she designs.

Her most recent venture is the nonprofit, *Your Time for Creative Empowerment, Inc.* Madona's desire to create an effective tool encompassing her professional skills as a visual and teaching artist and retired middle school teacher was the inspiration. The lessons she has learned from her life-experience as a mother, adult caregiver to parents in their nineties, a one-time divorcee/single mother navigating a contentious divorce, now a happily re-married woman to an attentive and supportive man are all part of this venture. She hopes to empower youth and families whose lives have been affected in similar ways and who are looking for creative self-help solutions to the twenty-first-century challenges and pitfalls.

Additionally, Madona's respect for the elderly and traditional cultures has pointed her in the direction of working with communities to engender cultural enrichment, respect for others–and in effect, unite communities throughout Long Island. She is thrilled about the opportunity and possibility of making a difference in this world, by using all of her God-given gifts and passionate heart in sharing the lessons she has learned to navigate life in her own creative way!

She has been able to navigate the obstacles accompanying divorce and the consequent single parenthood to provide solid educational experience and emotional support for her children who are now young adult college graduates. One is an aspiring Art Director with a bachelor's degree in Art and Design, and the other earned a bachelor's degree in Psychology and is currently pursuing a Master of Social Work Degree. Madona is thankful to God for giving her the strength and presence of mind to be an informed and passionate advocate for them within their schools, as well as the Family and Supreme Court systems.

Madona takes her community involvement potential with her wherever she goes by talking-the-talk and walking-the-walk. Having a comforting voice, she offers herself as a pillar of support to women, families, and children. Her participation in "paying it forward" to help others has emanated from her ability to passionately connect and empathize with people and life experiences. These life-lessons have taken her to places that validate her belief that we are all indeed our brothers'/sisters' "keepers," and we all have something to give, no matter how small, if only we would awaken the desire.

Her resulting mindset has been to approach life as a learning experience which must be put to good use in order that humanity may continue to thrive.

WORDS OF WISDOM

Despite her fair share of setbacks in life, Madona has been able to develop a presence of mind that has equipped her to rise above obstacles and understand how she can benefit from approaching such situations as opportunities to excel, rather than accept them as mechanisms to keep her down. HER TIME HAS COME!

It is her hope that she will in time, exemplify an exciting model for others in mixing business with compassion. She wants to be able to show that it is indeed alright for people to wear their hearts on their sleeves, and introduce meaningful, sensitive and compassionate practices into their business plans. That way, the reward will not only be financial, but it will also come with a component money cannot buy . . . LOVE.

QUESTIONS TO PONDER

- *What obstacles have you encountered that you can share with others?*
- *Who helps you navigate life?*
- *What life experiences have you had that can transform into good deeds?*
- *Have you had personal inspiration in your life that you can share with others?*
- *What was the most recent issue in your community you felt so strongly about, that you wished you had a say in it?*
- *If given the opportunity, what would you have done differently about it and why?*
- *What talents or training do you possess that you can use to help the underprivileged?*

CONNECT WITH MADONA

Email: madona@IConnectthedotsofcreativity.org

Websites: www.madonacoleoriginals.com

www.mytimehascome.org

www.yourtime4liny.org

www.Iconnectthedotsofcreativity.org

Phone: (516) 965-3242

Chapter Fourteen

NATURE CREATES ART

Vincent Smythe

"When you take your eyes off yourself and put them on someone else, your success becomes eminent. You will see your success when you help another reach theirs."

*V*incent has always loved nature; he has also loved any activity in the great outdoors. As a child growing up in the late 1950s and 1960s, he and the other kids would use their imaginations to make things from various found objects. He was always fascinated with wood, and once found some discarded pieces he used to make a tree house. Vincent's artistic ability came through loud and clear.

In fact, each person in his family was an artist of sorts. His mother wrote short stories and made stuffed animals and dolls, his father was a painter and commercial artist, so their talents were in Vincent's genes. His dad began working with fallen tree branches in the early to mid-1980s when he discovered a way to create art deco from those branches. He created his first art deco piece from a tree branch that was six feet long with other branches sprouting everywhere. He applied wood stain, paint and then added miniature artificial accessories like leaves, birds and a nest. That was his first tree-branch sculpture, and he hung it on the wall over the couch in his living room. When people came into his apartment they were amazed at what they saw.

Years later, Vincent began to create one-of-a-kind tree-branch art deco sculptures from his home studio. He created identifiable images such as people, birds and animal figures in full color made from tree branches in different sizes.

In late 2008, he had a full-time job in the insurance industry and was very unhappy. Going back to his roots by doing some soul searching, Vincent saw that all twigs pointed to his original gifts of working with art. He began to develop educational art curriculums meeting the required common-core learning standard for art education. He worked with groups to encourage them to interact with each other to improve their social skills by opening up dialogs and discussing the creative process. He highlighted their artistic abilities to help change the way they viewed nature in its natural form, at the same time helping these children, adults and seniors to be creative while using their minds.

These initiatives sprouted into teaching children and adults how to create the tree-branch sculptures in full color. Workshops that followed included 3-D Eco Art on Canvas, images of nature on canvas board, and a Caricature Plaque, which is the transfer of images onto a wood plaque. Vincent gave them the ability to connect with nature by experi-

> Going back to his roots by doing some soul searching, Vincent saw that all twigs pointed to his original gifts.

menting with new ways to create imaginary art in the twenty-first-century.

His students painted, traced, colored, and cut out animal images to attach to the canvas boards which had their own scenes from nature, whether it be a forest, ocean, farm or mountain setting and many others they worked on together.

Vincent's life work has branched off into his current mission that helps the environment, creates jobs and develops artistic skills. He is helping to preserve the environment through planting new trees in areas that have been destroyed by wildfires and violent storms. This campaign is known as "A Million Things to Do with a Tree" – creating an artistic tree to plant a new tree. It is supported by non-profit organizations, such as *Association for Helping Retarded Children* (AHRC) and *Disabled War Veterans* who hire men and women with mental and physical disorders. They help to create, manufacture and assemble the unfinished version of the Tree-Branch Sculpture Kit orders for individuals, schools and groups. Part of the proceeds goes toward planting new trees and creating necessary jobs for those who have some form of disability.

In addition, Vincent has partnered with *One World Ministries* in Brooklyn, NY to support an Anti-Bullying campaign and brand the Tree Branch Sculpture Kit using its signature Kangaroo, made from tree branches, as a national symbol.

Nature is universal and is used in many forms to ignite awareness and develop creative energy in all of us.

WORDS OF WISDOM

Over the years Vincent was able to transform his ideas into works of art. "Giving back in order to move forward shows humility and compassion for what you believe in. Let's give back to our earth by planting new trees to help save mother earth."

QUESTIONS TO PONDER

- *What can you do to help preserve your community?*
- *Have you ever created something from our earthly resources?*
- *Do you have a childhood experience with nature that can help others to be transformed?*

CONNECT WITH VINCENT

Email vincentfinebydesign@vincentfinebydesign.com

Website www.earthdayallday.com or www.alldayearthday.com

Phone 561.386.7194 (Palm Beach City, Florida)

Chapter Fifteen

GROW WHERE YOU ARE PLANTED

Nicholas Cariello

"Good, Better, Best.
Never let it rest, until your good is better, and better is Best."
~ St. Jerome

*M*y son Nicholas is very bright, creative, and has always been mature for his age. He has a passion and an innate ability for learning, along with great intuition and foresight for people and his surroundings. He has always connected with his teachers and in elementary school, became a teacher's helper. His favorite activity was "show and tell," and he would engage 100% of the students attention for the whole period. The teacher would come up to us, saying, "he's a 'natural,' and his presence lights up the room." His fourth-grade teacher, Miss Smith, encouraged him to try out for the school play, "*Grease*," where he played one of the T-Birds. His performance was spectacular, and the show was one of the best performances the school ever had. After seeing his love for theatre grow, we enrolled Nicholas in summer camp at The Stage in Merrick, now known as The Merrick Theatre and

Center for the Arts, a 501(c)3 nonprofit community theatre. The Theatre's formal mission is *"to benefit members of the community by providing education, entertainment, and exposure to cultural experiences."*

His acting abilities and love for the Theatre blossomed. The staff embraced him immediately and recognized his many natural talents. He originally got involved after Jeanine, the director of children's performances at the time, asked him, "Would you like to run sound for us?" He said, "Yes, why not!" That question eventually led to him volunteering to oversee the lighting, sound, and set components for every production at the Theatre. He earned the title of Production Director. He invests a large quantity of time into ensuring excellent production quality. He also makes it a point to put time and effort into each production to make sure each different director's vision comes to life onstage.

Nicholas says, "My motivation stems from my early childhood; my mother always encouraged me to take action and get involved. Her mantra is "be the best you can be and do the best you can do; you can do anything you put your mind to." Nicholas listens to my input and suggestions, and he is always interested in helping anyone and everyone. He is a very compassionate, kind, and caring person. At the Theatre, he saw a need, and he filled it. He's been there for eleven years, and has seen more needs and continues to fill them.

> We can impact many lives through our actions.

Joe Mauro, the Operations Director at the Theatre, and one of Nicholas' mentors, said, "Nicholas is my right hand man, and the best light designer and tech guy on Long Island. He believes in being a team player as well as being a team leader."

A driving factor for his motivation within the theatre is the reaction he gets to see from the audience. He loves getting to be a part of the magic that goes into making the production come to life, and its even more gratifying when he gets to see the audience become immersed in the story. His personal mission is a quote by Ghandi: "Be the change you want to see in the world." We can impact many lives through our actions; his actions make theatrical performances come to life.

After high school, Nicholas received the Presidents Scholarship to attend New York Tech, and majored in Computer Science. Like most freshman college students, Nicholas was trying to find his place. While going through that tough transition, Nicholas noticed there was no club for computer science. Once again, he saw a need and filled a need: Nicholas started the New York Tech Chapter of ACM (Association for Computing Machinery) in January 2017.

Throughout his time as founder and president, Nicholas was able to coordinate a trip to California with the club's executive board, lead students in seminars on current technology, and facilitate a six thousand dollar grant for the club. He was also given the amazing opportunity as a student leader on campus to network with fellow students, faculty, and leaders throughout the New York Tech community. He truly grew his roots at New York Tech and happily calls New York Tech, "a home away from home," even long after graduation.

Nicholas says, "Throughout my life, I've experienced many different 're-planting' moments. Those are the moments when you're faced with being cut from your garden and are then replanted elsewhere. With each replanting, I took the knowledge I had from the previous garden and put it to work growing roots in the next one. With New York Tech, I took my production and leadership experience from the Theatre and put it into practice as the lighting director for commencement."

Nicholas explains that in his 'replantings' he has found a common thread: the Theatre. He says, "The Theatre has been one of my strongest and most consistent growing points. I have always found that wherever I was, or whatever I was doing, it somehow tied back to the theater. For me, the most fruitful experience of the theater has been meeting the love of my life, Lindsey."

Nicholas also says, "I am most proud of my personal accomplishments alongside those at the theatre. Over the course of four years, I have worked on more than 200 productions and at the same time worked to earn my Bachelor's Degree (Cum Laude) as well as a Master's Degree (With Distinction), both in Computer Science. Volunteering in my community has not held me back; it has pushed me forward to succeed."

WORDS OF WISDOM

Working within the community gives you a sense of belonging. I feel so attached to the theatre and all that I do there. I would best compare my work at the theatre to a flower in a garden; you carefully water it, make sure it gets enough sunlight, and over the years, your flower grows and grows and grows. It is just so rewarding to watch the community benefit right before your eyes.

QUESTIONS TO PONDER

- How have activities you began as a child impacted your life as an adult?

- How can you encourage your children to follow their passion?
- How can you help your children get involved in community activities?
- Are you letting your children be their true selves?

CONNECT WITH NICHOLAS

Email: nfcariello@gmail.com

Merrick Theatre and Center for the Arts

Website: www.merrick-theatre.com

Chapter Sixteen

DIFFERENT ABILITIES COME TO LIFE

Christine Keller, M.A., M.S.Ed.

"The good we secure for ourselves is precarious and uncertain until it is secured for all of us and incorporated into our common life."
~Jane Addams

As a child/teen in the '70s, social justice issues were in the air. Activism was in Christine Keller's blood since early childhood. Much of her inspiration came from the film *Free to Be You and Me* with Marlo Thomas, which was shown in their elementary school by progressive educators. She had a vision of starting a learning center for children.

Christine is the mother of son, Sage, and daughter, Samaya, and is married to a wonderful man named Craig. Her children's names reflect her commitment to the path of wisdom. Time would reveal the birth of Sage as the birth of true wisdom, and through Samaya, she would learn the patience to endure the ebb and flow of this new path her life's journey has taken.

Sage was a very happy yet very intense baby. From about 15 months old, Christine recognized that something was up. He would get easily overstimulated and developed vocal and motor tics. He exhibited impulsive behavior, especially in social settings. And he had to have everything "exactly" in its place and clean. Christine recognized the signs of ADHD and OCD and learned about sensory integration disorder over time.

At home, Sage flourished. A very bright child, he enjoyed watching the History and Biography Channels and loved geography. Using his many maps and globes, Christine created a daily *learn while we play* routine with her son, which led to her choice of Montessori's stimulating environment for preschool.

At their first parent-teacher conference, the teacher said, "Sage excels in geography, but learns while under the table throwing things." With no guidance to offer

> IMAGINE . . . an education that challenges and inspires, honors your child's individuality . . .

and the glare of judgment that so many parents of children like Sage have seen, Christine decided to move him to a different classroom with a more understanding teacher. This teacher suggested she read a book about Sensory Integration Disorder, *The Out of Sync Child* by Carol Kranowitz. She then suggested Sage be evaluated through the public school. Sage experienced many challenges in school that were either compounded by or resolved through his teachers' level of compassion and skill.

After much research and many contentious school meetings, Christine became an advocate for her son, dealing with every challenge and educating her family along the way. She went back to school for her second master's in childhood education/special education. It was a journey that took them to a school where the principal, educators, and staff embraced the Collaborative & Proactive Solutions approach, transforming

Sage's life. He became more active and felt part of a community, which kept him moving in a positive direction.

Christine also vowed to help others and NEVER have another parent go through the painful experiences she and Sage had endured. Her "Wolf Spirit" had been sparked. She says, "this is the identity that manifests in many moms when their children are at risk; it is the protective instinct to come to the aid of all children when their lives are in harm's way, whether unintentional or otherwise."

Over time, Christine's organization, *The Children's Sangha*, was born, offering programs and services for children and young adults, as well as a community support group for parents where both can be understood, accepted, and guided, building a collaborative community. Her journey on behalf of her children turned into a journey on behalf of ALL children.

After graduating from high school, Sage was accepted into college and is majoring in Media and Communications, minoring in Environmental Studies. He has a job, a car, friends and is enjoying LIFE! He and Samaya are not just siblings, but great friends! Christine's family is whole, having weathered the ebb and flow and continuing to help others in the process.

The goals of *The Children's Sangha* continue as they reach out to greater numbers within the community, highlighting the fact that we all have "Different Abilities" to be embraced and cultivated. The Children's Sangha slogan is *"Where Different Abilities Come to Life!"* Its mission is to plant seeds of stewardship in children and young adults by deepening their understanding of themselves, others, and nature, as well as fostering the spirit of education in adults and joys of growing a mind that they may cultivate in our youth. They are happy to say that their stewardship and mentoring programs, as well as community services, have impacted many.

Parents have stated that the kids have lots of fun participating in *The Children's Sangha* while gaining knowledge, independence, and self-esteem. *The Children's Sangha* is also a most valuable resource to parents. They help parents to navigate through the school system by identifying services that will benefit their child and stand beside them as services are implemented. NO parent has to go through this process alone. Their upbeat attitude brings out the best in families.

Christine's vision of starting a learning center for children has become her reality. The newly established Sangha Education Center—*A Place of Wonder* is a non-profit 501c-3 to be located in a historic home that they will be sharing with community partners who embrace their vision for "heart-centered learning." They look forward to opening their doors and hearts to the Long Island community at large.

IMAGINE . . . an education that challenges and inspires, honors your child's individuality, nurtures mutual respect, fosters relationship building, connects community . . . an education without labels, without limits! Through her journey, Christine has enabled our youth to value themselves and be valued as members of the Earth community.

WORDS OF WISDOM

Focus on those abilities that are often not being cultivated and the needs not being fully met. As Nelson Mandela stated: "The true character of society is revealed in how it treats its children." Systems tend to blame the victims. We need to take the emphasis off "lack" or "weakness" and place it on "strength" and "ability." What is evident is that when using a strength-based approach to learning or working with our youth and developing the innate abilities within each individual, they soar.

QUESTIONS TO PONDER

- *What does "stewardship" mean to you and how can you incorporate the meaning of this word in your life?*
- *Does the idea of social action resonate with you?*
- *What cause or injustice motivates you to take action?*
- *How will you become an action-oriented individual?*
- *Do you believe that children are our future?*
- *How can you help to address any one or more of the issues facing today's kids and the systemic issues that lead to limited outcomes?*

CONNECT WITH CHRISTINE:

www.thechildrenssangha.com/contact/   or   christine@thechildrenssangha.com

"You will not be punished for your anger; you will be punished by your anger." ~ *Buddha*

*E*ileen Lichtenstein, a business owner, educator and life/career success coach, has utilized her expertise and experiences for many years to help empower individuals and organizations to reach the pinnacles of their success and productivity. Through coaching and group facilitation locally and across the country, she teaches people how to become centered, and shows them how to tap into their own inner strength to attain life and business success.

Eileen has always been innovative and an "out-of-the-box" thinker. Self-expression and improved communication was integrated into her life even at the tender age of three when she learned she could communicate non-verbally through dance. She believes dance helped her make a real connection to mind and body and opened the door to unlimited possibilities.

Aside from helping people through her business, she became

involved in community outreach years ago, beginning with volunteerism at the *Long Island Works Coalition*. There, she helped students become motivated about career choices, she also assisted at career fairs in middle schools and high schools throughout Long Island. Eileen was motivated to make a difference in the community when she noticed a lack of intergenerational services, as well as her acknowledgment of distinctions to support better communication–and techniques to reduce stress/frustration.

Later, Eileen worked with the National Alliance for the Mentally Ill (NAMI) in recovery and community outreach groups, and eventually became a skilled Anger-Management Practitioner for the courts-mandated training certification program. Additionally, Eileen provided workshops to those who have been traumatized by Sandy, the devastating storm that hit Long Island and New Jersey in October 2012.

> When you believe in yourself and love yourself unconditionally, others will too!

Today, Eileen empowers people to be the best they can be. She has observed that empowerment and self-esteem are all that an individual needs to move forward and positively change their personal and professional lives.

Perhaps the most rewarding accomplishment in Eileen's life has been the production of three electronic books and an audio program, as well as building a business that reaches across generations and provides services in the areas she feels passionate about–stress/anger management and effective communication for her community. She has been a shining light of hope for those willing to ASK for HELP.

Eileen continually strives to "be part of the force for good in the world."

WORDS OF WISDOM

It has often been Eileen's observation that the missing link in getting past blocks and moving forward is improved self-esteem and empowerment. When you believe in yourself and love yourself unconditionally, others will too!

QUESTIONS TO PONDER

- *Are you ready to Boost your Self Esteem and Boost your Life?*
- *What actions can you take today to enrich your life?*
- *Do you have an experience in your life that opened a door to your inner strength?*
- *In what ways do you empower others?*

CONNECT WITH EILEEN

Email: Eileeen@balanceandpower.com

Website: www.balanceandpower.com

Phone: (516) 623-4353

Chapter Eighteen

THE REWARDS ARE PRICELESS AND ENDLESS

Patricia Block

"Live, love, laugh, and live in the moment.
Take time to meditate and rest your busy minds, bodies, and souls."

*P*atricia Block is a special education teacher at General Douglas MacArthur High School in Levittown. She is the wife of a kind, caring man named Alan, and the mother of two amazing, humble young adults—a son Nicholas and a daughter Nicole. Her family is her first passion; her second is helping others in need. That's why she became a volunteer for many different organizations that have moved her into action, including: *"The Heather on Earth Music Foundation,"* which offers music therapy to children in hospitals, soothing them as they heal. The founder of the organization was a dear friend of Patricia's, who passed away recently, and the memories of Patricia and her friend at various children's hospitals . . . crafting, singing, and passing out toys, remains ingrained in her mind.

With the help of her students, who also overcame huge obstacles in their lives, Patricia wrote and illustrated a children's book in memory of her friend Geri and Geri's youngest daughter, Heather, who passed away at a very young age from a malignant brain tumor. Patricia will have the book published this year.

She is a staunch believer in the philosophy that every person can make a difference in the lives of those less fortunate. To this end, she teaches her students how to volunteer by organizing programs that serve many different charities. Children from kindergarten through fifth grade took part in her recycling program. This endeavor not only taught the children the value of helping others, but it also spilled over into their home lives, showing their parents and friends the relevance of their actions. It thrills her to watch her students volunteer on their own for causes they have become passionate about. Patricia raised thousands of dollars for many causes in their community by getting her students involved in recycling and helping to create a local fundraiser.

"Volunteering is a legacy; we can never tell where or when our influence stops."

Since her toddler years, and continuing through her childhood, adolescent, and adulthood, she has been driven to help others. Patricia remembers being in Coney Island with her grandmother when at the tender age of three, she handed half her sandwich to a homeless woman who was foraging the garbage for food. It is a memory she'll never forget. After seeing the positive outcome of that incident, and later in helping others, she has been determined to do even more.

Patricia takes pride in her accomplishments, most of all her children's personal academic and private achievements, and the work she has completed over the years helping others to have better lives. As a parent and teacher, she has always made it a priority to study, play an instrument, be active in sports, and volunteer to fulfill personal happiness. In addition to having empathy for others, the tools and skills she has applied are leadership, honesty, and hard, persistent work. The work she has done and continues to do brings her priceless compensation.

"Volunteering is a legacy; we can never tell where or when our influence stops."

Patricia's recommendation to others is to find a cause that makes you happy and brings you enjoyment, or something you are passionate about. Then get involved. It will change your life forever.

Recently, Patricia had to come to terms with losing her mother-in-law. Who lived a healthy and long life, passing away at age 99. She knitted the most magnificent sweaters made from the finest yarns and accessorized with authentic buttons. Patricia and her daughter will share them and wear them proudly in her memory for years to come. They cherish the time spent with her, even toward the end of her life. They took her to her favorite eatery, and Patricia's husband did his mom's grocery shopping every week.

Aging was a scary thought for Nettie ("Mom" is what Patricia always called her) and my 89-year-old mother. She invited them both to live with us in her home, promising them that they would never live out their last days in a nursing home. Patricia's sister and two brothers take turns transporting their mom to doctor appointments, shopping for her, and keeping her company and they hired a full-time, live-in nursing aide to care for her.

"We need to embrace and care for our elderly as they once cared for us."

WORDS OF WISDOM

"I empathize with children or adults who are less fortunate and hurting in some way – and it touches my heart, compelling me to help them in ANY way that I can. This drives me to get involved directly with causes that are dear to me," says Patricia. *"By touching the lives of people in my community, the rewards are endless. When people are able to see other people do beneficial and kind things for others, they too want to be kind."*

QUESTIONS TO PONDER

- *In what ways can you help a less fortunate child or adult?*
- *What are you doing in your life to be a role model?*
- *Are you fulfilling your life purpose?*

CONNECT WITH PATTY:

Email: Patty818@aol.com

Phone: (516) 225-4703

THE BIG BAD BOOT

Valentina Janek

"Get up! Get dressed! Show up! Never Give Up!"

a t a young age, Valentina was taught by her parents to always give back. Even though her parents didn't have much, they always found a way to help others. Watching her parents give to others, even during their difficulties, made a lasting impression on her and it would carry into her adult life. One of the most important lessons she learned from her mom was to respect others. As far back as she can remember, Valentina's mom never had a bad word to say about anyone, no matter what the circumstances. Her mom taught her to look for the good in everyone and respect their individualism. She believes it is important to help others, not only for them but also for herself. Her baby sister, Maria, always said, *"What goes around comes around. You get what you give. So be KIND!"*

. . .

Will Rogers once said, *"Even if you are on the right track, you'll get run over if you just sit there."* You see, Valentina was on the right track; she had her corporate job and was very comfortable. It wasn't until she was fired from her long-standing job at age fifty, that she realized there were so many others just like her, who were left to "fend for themselves" in regards to getting back into the workforce. Even though she had been giving back to her community since childhood, she decided it was time to take "giving back" up a notch.

The patriarch of her family known, as "Papa," would always say: *"The power of the mind can do wonderful things."* He instilled in her that no matter what obstacle

"They say in the end, all that really matters are the connections and relationships people share."

would come your way, they were to remain standing. That's why she speaks words of encouragement to her daughter, her grandchildren, and anyone else she comes in contact with! So, after the hurt, disappointment, tears, lots of ice cream nights, self-reflection, and encouragement from those around her, she decided it was time to take this negative life-altering experience and turn it into something positive, not only for herself but for others going through similar situations. She arranged to have a meet up at the Sweet Hollow Diner for breakfast with other unemployed mid-lifers. She met up with Joanne, Patricia, Stephanie, and Chris, whom she met while going on interviews, and they became co-founders of the club. The five started meeting week after week, strategizing ways that they could get a job.

Once again, they got the big bad boot; this time from the diner, because they weren't spending enough money and were taking up too much space. The group decided to take things into their own hands. Valentina started the club as a joke, having been on so many interviews and told she was too experienced, had an income they would not consider, and was "too old"–without them saying it. They convinced themselves to become entrepreneurial and started *The Long Island Breakfast Club*, *(LIBC)*, which was founded in 2006. Their goal was to help middle class "fifty-plus" mid-life Long Islanders pave the way back into the workforce. But as the club grew, so did their goals. For over thirteen years, *LIBC* has been providing career counseling, support, and advocacy for experienced, in-transition professionals, referrals, companionship, business networking, contacts for interviewing, and mentors to all Long Islanders to help them succeed. The club has a saying: *"We Meet, We Eat, We Seek"* ... a "socialpreneurship" they call it. *LIBC* provides an opportunity for local business owners, representatives of local businesses, men & women seeking jobs/careers to come together over a delicious meal and network! Their motto is: *"Philotimo! Experience impacts the world beyond imagination!"*

Unfortunately, she would face more heartache with the loss of Joanne Fiorentino Lucas co-founder of LIBC to ovarian cancer and her baby sister Maria Rosa Petrowski to breast cancer, who was also a Floral Park legend and a club member, loved by many members.

> *"If you sit back and let the game pass you by, that is how your life will be."*
>
> ~Joanne Fiorentino Lucas~

Even though Valentina has lost important people in her life, she used her experience of those losses to help others once again.

Her loss catapulted *LIBC* into not only being about helping people with jobs but about helping people with any need. When her dear friend Joanne passed away from ovarian cancer, The *LIBC* put together a big event and raised a lot of money in Joanne's honor to the fight against ovarian cancer. After her baby sister passed away, the Pietrowski family created *"RIA's Angels,"* and each year, *Breakfast Club* members attend their fundraising event in memory of Maria to help support the fight against breast cancer.

One club member, Macky, lost her niece, Lisa Eberle, at a young age. Lisa loved Christmas, so in her memory, *LIBC* started a program *"Lisa Eberle Toy Drive"* that gives presents to children whose families can't afford to give them presents. The club then teamed up with her good friend, Diana, who volunteered at the *Long Island Volunteer Center*, whose mission is to promote volunteerism and to improve the quality of life across Long Island. Diana and Valentina were the visionaries behind making Bethpage State Park home to the *"LI Bench Program."* Even through all her pain, Valentina always finds a way to start over again, or create something new through sharing her experience, strength, and hope with as many people as possible.

As you can see, the *Long Island Breakfast Club* has made a difference in our community and beyond by continuously extending helping hands. Valentina believes volunteering is good for your soul, career, health, and social endeavors, and it will lead to success in your personal and business life. With all that has happened, she and the club remain standing!

She has always been an advocate for her community and the needs of those around her. Valentina looks back with gratitude to the corporate job because she realized very quickly that the best day of the rest of her life was that day, as it gave her wings to fly! She published *"From Fired To Freedom: How Life After The Big, Bad Boot Gave Me Wings.* Her book launch and signing happened on the first anniversary of her husband's passing, a goal she made during his illness, knowing he would be passing in a few weeks. This book is a compilation of inspirational, engaging, and funny stories from Valentina and many other members of the *Breakfast Club* who received the "pink slip" or experienced another major life change but came out on the other side better and brighter for it.

Valentina's book led to the collaboration with Stephanie at *Red Penguin Books* and me with the *Long Island Way.* Together we started the *"Long Island Writers Club."* We believe "Everyone Has A Story...Write That Book." The *Writer's Club* aims to provide instruction, support, accountability, encouragement, community, and celebration to future and accomplished authors. Everyone has a story. How true it is!

Dubbed as the Long Island "It Girl," Valentina's lifelong dream and vision was to host a radio talk show one day. She answered the call by saying yes to stand up comedy with other want-to-be comedians. She didn't realize this would lead her to host her radio talk show on Govs Radio "The Long Island Breakfast Club – Tina Valentina Show." She has expanded the club's reach to give a voice to club members and others on the live streaming platform. She calls it the show about everything and nothing. Guests come on to talk about their business, jobs, resources, and sharing information of use to others. There are conversations about hobbies, announcements of grand open-ings of local restaurants and theatrical shows, including performers at local clubs, whether they be acting, singing, danc-ing, or comedy. She introduces them to the listeners/viewers all over Long Island.

Valentina feels lucky, blessed, and confident that her time has come to be able to do this wonderful work. She says "Believe me, I do believe that life is full of possibilities, and anything can happen if you continue to believe."

"They say in the end, all that really matters are the connections and relationships people share. When people come together simply due to similar circumstances, things happen."

~Valentina~

Valentina believes there are three things we all should do every day:

1. Laugh. Laughter is the best medicine.

2. Think. Spend some time in thought or quiet contemplation.

3. Let your emotions be free. If you need to cry, then cry.

It doesn't matter if they're tears of sadness or tears of happiness. Just think about it... If you've laughed, thought, and cried, all in one day, that's a full day! Actually, that's a heck of a day! And if you're doing that seven days a week, that means you're going to have something special!

WORDS OF WISDOM

Valentina wants to encourage you to surround yourself with people who are smarter than you, so you'll always be hungry to learn more.

Get involved with a community project that you've never done before.

Make sure to have fun. Step out of your comfort zone!

Enjoy your life & the precious moments you have.

Follow her three "To Do's" and be enthusiastic every day… Ralph Waldo Emerson said, *"Nothing great was ever achieved without enthusiasm."*

Keep your dreams alive despite whatever problems you may have. Work hard for your dreams, and push to make them come true!

You have a gift; it's time to share that gift with others!

Valentina says you've got to *"Get up! Get dressed! Show up! Never Give Up!"*

QUESTIONS TO PONDER

- *Where do you see a need that you can fill in your community?*
- *Is there a group, program, or person that helped you during a time of need? Ask them how you can give back.*
- *If you were going through a difficult time in your life and you knew someone that had a need that wasn't being met, would you help that person?*

"Never doubt that a small group of thoughtful, committed citizens can change the world; indeed, it's the only thing that ever has."
~Margaret Mead

• • •

Connect with Valentina:

Email: *VJanek@optonline.net*

FB: *Facebook.com/ValentinaJanek*

Facebook.com/LongIslandBreakfastClub

www.longislandbreakfastclub.org

www.valentinajanek.com

SECTION III

*We Stand United
in Spirit*

Chapter Twenty

GIVE WITHOUT STRINGS ATTACHED

Mary Zelenak

"Green Tara is my spiritual mother, and her mantra is: OM TARA TUITARE TURE SOHA. She will come swiftly if you call on her. Mantras are mind protectors. We are always looking to protect our mind."

*M*ary, also known as Kelsang Sangwang, is a Buddhist Nun who lived upstate at the Temple in Glen Spey, New York for three years. She has been a nun for over ten years, teaching and helping others, and finding their inner qualities. Mary is a therapist by profession and facilitates many spiritual groups to help people find their spiritual path.

Her life took a turn when she went out on disability from her job as an Addiction Counselor in NYC. She found herself in need of some guidance and direction and was looking for a meditation practice. Looking through *Creations Magazine*, she found a mediation class in Huntington, which was within walking distance from her home. There she was introduced to her first Buddhist teacher and she has been practicing ever since. She loves the belief system of the Buddhist tradition, *"Happiness is within and everything is about the mind; some people call this the Spirit."* Mary has been teaching Buddhism for more than ten years. Living at the temple has given her the opportunity to help many people enjoy the lovely grounds and find peace of mind. In her private work, she helps people to go within and find the true source of their happiness or pain.

Mary's own pain is what motivated her to reach out for help. She knew there was a better way to live and sought it out–and then helped others to do the same. From that point on, her personal mission was to help as many people as she could, as well as to understand that there is no happiness outside of our minds–the happiness we are seeking is right inside each of us.

Many years ago, Mary became involved in community outreach programs, and then decided to go to college for recreation therapy

> We can give without strings attached.

where she began working with the mental health population. It was hard work and she was unhappy with the way the staff treated these individuals. There were so many addicted clients, and nobody was addressing this issue. So, she went to South Oaks and took the addiction-counseling course to be able to do something about it. She then began her work in the field at South Oaks Hospital and many other agencies. It was through working with those suffering in addiction that she recognized the pain in people, and that there was no way out but to go within.

Mary's biggest accomplishment in her life has been her two daughters. Motherhood did not come easy for her but her love for them has never changed. They have been her greatest teachers. Her second accomplishment has been her own ability to change, and to continue to change, to become a better person and help others to do the same. What gives her the most pride is her co-dependency recovery–it has changed her life. She has been fortunate enough to be able to help others change their lives in this area as well.

One of Mary's goals is to become interdependent, which is different than co-dependent. Interdependency is pure love; we are not dependent on things outside ourselves for our own happiness. We can give without strings attached.

WORDS OF WISDOM

Mary believes we truly find happiness by looking within ourselves and knowing that it has always been there. Go for it and trust your spiritual self. The truth will set you free.

QUESTIONS TO PONDER

- *Do you have a mantra that you live by?*
- *Are you giving without strings attached?*
- *Do you realize that everything you need is right inside of yourself?*

CONTACT MARY

Email: jnjsnannyz@yahoo.com

Chapter Twenty-One

TIME TO HAVE A VOICE

Maria Studer

"You will never feel 100 percent ready when an opportunity arises."
Quoted by many wise people.

*M*aria, a Presbyterian Ruling Elder, active in her congregation and in the wider denomination, had retired from teaching Italian for thirty-five years to junior high school students on Long Island, New York. Over the years, she had volunteered her time in school, church and several other organizations. For several years, she coordinated a "bell-ringing" campaign in her church whose members united with other churches and community groups in the Levittown area to raise money for the Salvation Army at holiday time. In addition, she led several work trips from her church to help post-Katrina, New Orleans in the recovery and rebuilding effort.

In retirement she has been given the opportunity to become involved in two issues that are very important to her–advocacy for our Lesbian, Gay, Bi-sexual and Transgender (LGBT) community. Specifically, advocacy and help in the integration of our immigrant community.

She originally became involved in this work when her Pastor suggested that she attend a meeting of a denominational group that was working to change the attitudes and church regulations of the LGBT ordination. In her role as LGBT advocate, she became a member of the Pride-in-the-Pulpit program of the Empire State Pride Agenda where church leaders advocate for LGBT rights. She also joined both the NY State Pride Agenda and the Long Island Transgender Advocacy programs, working towards initiating a civil rights law to protect the members of our transgender community. Her work in these groups, primarily on Long Island with yearly trips to the state capital to lobby, involved meetings and phone calls, collecting signatures and contacting legislators.

Getting involved was easy. The road was paved for her to gain a voice and be heard. She had friends and acquaintances in committed relationships who

> Maria is always reminded that one drop at a time is how the bucket is filled.

were members of the LGBT community; and her faith led her to believe that this work was right, necessary, and was the next step in the "bending of the arc of history towards justice." When Pride in the Pulpit became active in her area, she was contacted and became involved. This organization was comprised of a group of church leaders, representing many religions, working for justice for the LGBT community.

As a member of Pride in the Pulpit, Maria advocated for an anti-discrimination law for students (Dignity for All Students), a Marriage Equality law and a Transgender Civil Rights law (GENDA). The first two were signed into law. Her faith, her ethics and her upbringing taught her that everyone is entitled to be respected, and when respect and/or civil rights are denied to anyone, we are all diminished.

In the role of immigrant advocate, she was a member of the Board of the Dowling College Center for Intergenerational Policy and Practice, and as such, she volunteered to coordinate a tutoring program that trains college students and community volunteers to teach English as a Second Language as well as prepare adult immigrants for the U.S. Citizenship Test. She also periodically teaches the classes with her tutors. These programs are in Suffolk County, New York.

Maria became involved in the ESL/Citizenship work as a result of her daughter's experience in a Temple University intergenerational program called Project SHINE (Students Helping in the Naturalization of Elders.) She immediately thought her immigrant community on Long Island would benefit from this program as would the college students. Her daughter certainly was benefitting from it. So, she called the director of the Temple program to get information about how someone would go about setting up one on Long Island. As luck or providence would have it, their former assistant director was giving a presentation on the program at a local conference. After the conference, Maria spoke with the director at length, she decided to pursue the creation of a program on Long Island.

After meeting with the agency representatives, it was decided her tutors would help in two existing classes. Maria then needed to train more tutors and volunteers. Her daughter helped to construct a training program like SMILE, and with the help of another Dowling College volunteer, they trained students and got started with a six-week pilot program. By that fall they had expanded to another agency and were running some of their own classes—and by the fall of 2012 they had expanded to a third agency.

She remained an active member of that intergenerational group as a new director was named. The group morphed into the Dowling College Center for Intergenerational Policy and Practice, as well as the Long Island Chapter of the New York State Intergenerational Network.

They are currently in the sixth year of the program. They are self-funded through personal donations from tutors and retired community volunteers. The classes are generally small and, as you may have guessed, a drop in the bucket in terms of the enormous need; but Maria is always reminded that one drop at a time is how the bucket is filled.

Since her program is based on Temple University's Project SHINE, she hopes one day to become part of their consortium. There is a fee involved, and they have no budget, no salaries—basically no money. That dream will entail getting at least one grant, which is the next challenge. Fortunately, many of the teaching materials are available online at no cost. Maria wanted to do something that might make the world a little better for others. Remember it may not work out exactly as you envision, so be flexible but stick to the dream.

WORDS OF WISDOM

Starting anything has always frightened Maria, e.g. making mistakes, not being thought well of, not being ready and generally, not feeling as competent as other people believe her to be. Instead of listening to the fright, Maria chooses to push past the fear and move forward anyway.

If you have something in mind, the questions below may help you to get closer to your vision.

QUESTIONS TO PONDER

- *What is it you want to do? Why?*
- *What are the steps you need to take to make it happen? (Education "formal or informal," contacts, mentor, others with more expertise than you have, and money).*
- *With whom do you need to network in order to gain credibility, get the word out, or set up the project?*
- *If funding is necessary, how will you get it? (Grants, donations, loans, etc.)*

CONTACT MARIA

Email: rstuder@optonline.net

Website for ESL / Citizenship program:

sites.google.com / site / longislandesl /

Phone: 516-840-5678

Chapter Twenty-Two

IGNITING SOCIAL JUSTICE

Amit Sur

"Stop acquiring more useless toys; dedicate some portion of your time to provide a helping hand to others. Your life will change. I promise you."

Amit's life took a 360-degree turn when he became involved in community service. Two outstanding individuals were the inspiration behind his own active work with volunteerism. One was very well-known for her philanthropy and spiritualism–Mother Teresa; and the other person was a close friend and disciple of Mahatma Gandhi–his maternal grandfather, Hanseswar Roy. Their true love of people and the principles by which they lived are a constant source of encouragement to him.

Amit is active in several initiatives to help people in need, coordinated by his parish–the Unitarian Universalist Congregation at Shelter Rock, Manhasset. He also took it upon himself to reach out to the community in other ways by becoming the

Chairman of his congregation's membership committee and, in this role, held events at the facility to introduce members to many nonprofits so they would gain a better understanding of the charity's missions and activities.

Amit's own mission is an honorable one: he speaks at religious institutions throughout Long Island about the life and message of Mahatma Gandhi and Mother Teresa *"who worked tirelessly for the improvement of the lives of poor people."* This work contributes to his own personal growth, as he is gratified to know that his efforts inspire attendees to get involved in community outreach.

The Board of Trustees at the Unitarian Universalist Congregation at Shelter Rock, (UUCSR) with Amit's support, has positively impacted the lives of many.

> He feels that everyone should be aware that "we are in it together."

One such initiative of this organization involved the creation of a Large Grant Program. Through this commendable program, the congregation has given grants to various nonprofit organizations, including The Interfaith Nutrition Network in Hempstead (INN), Family Service League in Huntington, The Nassau County Coalition Against Domestic Violence, Mental Health Association of Nassau County in Hempstead, and many other organizations.

Amit also personally supports The Long Island Way community because he relates strongly to that organization's mission–to have nonprofit organizations and for-profit companies work together for their mutual benefit. This innovative concept brings awareness, funding and gives community-minded individuals the opportunity to network and help one another.

His involvement with nonprofits, especially the INN, has positively impacted his life, and perhaps, his future. *"This is an exceptional organization that treats each of its guests with dignity and care."* His efforts with this organization inspired other members of the UUCSR to give their time to assist this important charity. Members of the congregation prepare soup for those less fortunate at the INN, as their way of *"paying it forward."*

One of Amit's favorite quotes is attributed to Jesus Christ who said, *"Love one another. As I have loved you—so you must love one another."* This truly seems to be the way Amit lives his own life, as evidenced by his work with the community.

WORDS OF WISDOM

Amit's day job is in the Financial Services Industry where he has learned an important life-lesson about the significance of giving back. He feels that everyone should be aware that *"we are in it together."* What this means to him is that people of all backgrounds can enjoy a peaceful life together if they take action, whether it's in a big way or a small way—and help each other, especially those who need basic necessities such as food, shelter, and health care.

QUESTIONS TO PONDER

- *Can you help your community by supplying food to the food bank?*
- *How can you spread the word to help a nonprofit or charity?*
- *How can you contribute to living a peaceful life?*
- *Fill in the Blank: "Together We Can*

  _____!*

CONNECT WITH AMIT

email: amit.sur@gmail.com

Chapter Twenty-Three

ST. THERESE LIVES ON

Rose Orefice

"The little flower within this hour show your power to help me and guide me." ~ Rose's Daily Prayer

*E*very year since 1945, they've celebrated on the first Sunday of October "The Feast Day" at the Little Flower Shrine of St Therese.

The three sisters, Joanne, a.k.a. Jerry and Rosalie, a.k.a. Bobby and Rose committed to donating their time, money, and resources to the Little Flower Shrine located in Hauppauge, Long Island, founded by Josephine Martello. Josephine was a very dedicated Catholic who wanted to join the convent, to serve God like St. Therese. The guidance and direction she received was that obedience is better than sacrifice.

Josephine married Bartholomew, a wonderful man, and before the birth of her son John, she was afflicted with an illness that gave her symptoms of epilepsy. She was told not to worry; it was probably due to her pregnancy. She then battled abdominal infections and became very ill for 13 years. During that time, St. Therese would come to her through her dreams. Then, one night, she got a surge of strength as she sat up in bed and started to pray for St. Therese to intercede, not for her but for her children, who needed a mother, and for her husband. She promised that she would go around and beg from all her friends until she raised enough money to build a little shrine on her property in honor of St. Therese. Then she went back to sleep again.

In another dream, St. Therese was smiling at her; and she said, "St. Therese, all my life I've wanted to serve you, all my life I've wanted to help the sick." St. Therese

> She lives a life of service to others because it makes her feel good.

responded, "Josephine, you will help the sick. I will send them to you. I will give you the strength. I will give you the power. I will, Josephine, I will, I will, I will." From that day forward, her healing process began, and no matter what, Josephine ALWAYS HAD FAITH.

Rose's sister, Jerry's son, Alfred, was very sick with a stomach disorder and was unable to keep food down. Jerry's friend, Millie, told her about the miracles of The Shrine of St. Therese, the Little Flower. Millie's sister was Josephine Martello, who fulfilled her promise to build a shrine dedicated to St. Therese in her backyard. Alfred spent two weeks receiving prayers and a special diet with Josephine and her family. Alfred was cured! He was one of the 44 miracle cures that happened that year.

From 1945 till now, Rose has been committed and devoted to St. Therese and The Feast Day, which gave her a passion and purpose beyond words. She was able to share her passion with her family and friends. The feast day was a big celebration. Hundreds of people gathered together to pray at the shrine. Then everyone would sit around the picnic area with their families enjoying conversation, food, and participating in the raffle prizes by buying chances to win Saint statues and 500 other gifts.

From January to October, Rose, Jerry, and Bobby were the fundraising committee and event coordinators; they donated their time, packing, wrapping and rolling in preparation for the big Feast Day! The money they raised with the raffle prizes helped pay for the upkeep of the shrine all these years.

Josephine Martello passed on October 13, 1989; her daughter, Sally, created a video of her and the book, *My Story*, by Josephine Martello. Sally and her children were able to continue Josephine's work at the Little Flower Shrine, helping people all over the world. Sally had an angelic spirit and a contagious smile.

Josephine's granddaughter, Sally's daughter, Theresa, told Rose what the Little Flower Shrine means to her; " St. Therese is a beautiful, loving, and healing blessing from the heavens, which is always in our hearts and showers us with her radiant abundance of colorful roses."

Rose created an altar she calls a mini shrine of St. Therese in her home. Family and friends would call her and ask her to pray to St. Therese for them. She writes a note with their prayer requests and places it on St. Therese's heart, so she can answer their prayers. Rose then prays, "May the little flower answer all your prayers and make your wishes come true."

Rose is very proud of her care-taking ability. She is always willing and able to help others. It comes naturally to her. She lives a life of service to others because it makes her feel good to serve.

WORDS OF WISDOM

Rose prays that for all of us to always continue to have faith and never give up. NO MATTER WHAT HAPPENS, have a good outlook. God is number one in her life, and her favorite Saint is the Little Flower, St. Therese. She believes people who have faith should continue to pray.

QUESTIONS TO PONDER

- *Do you have a family tradition you can continue for your family legacy?*
- *Who in your family could be part of your team?*
- *Do you have a daily prayer or affirmation you say everyday?*

CONNECT WITH

The Little Flower Shrine, 184 Roosevelt Blvd., Hauppage, NY 11788

Phone: 631-582-4122

Chapter Twenty-Four

INSPIRED GREETINGS FROM SEOUL TO SOUL

Jean Marie Prince

"If you believe in what you are doing and if it is good for the human race, then do it and do not let negative people stop you from it."

*J*ean Marie Prince, the author of the book *"Inspired Blessings" Led by God to Inspire the World with Love, Faith, and Hope,* has done exactly that! She was born in Seoul, Korea, and abandoned at two days old in a public bathroom at a train station. Adopted by an American family when she was five years old, she believes with all her heart that God saved her both physically and spiritually to share His love with everyone. Today, Jean Marie is a loving wife, mother of two, a joyful grandmother, and lives with her family in Long Island, NY, where she continues to spread the word of God's love through her writings.

She took a leap of faith in the fall of 2010 when she heard the Holy Spirit tell her to do the book! Inspired by these words of wisdom from the Spirit of God, she didn't question it, and told Him, *"You are right!"* Jean Marie never hesitated and a year later self-published her book. She also entered a national writing contest in 2012 and was given the National Indie Excellence® Award as a "Finalist for Short Stories 2012."

Jean Marie, also a songwriter, produced three CD Albums called *"Inspired Blessings" Songs by Jean Marie Prince* in 2015, 2017, and *Little "Inspired Blessings" God's Delightful Child* in 2018. Since 2013 she has produced her Christian TV Talk Show called "Inspired Blessings with Jean Marie Prince." She has also been sharing her amazing testimony at churches, on TV, on radio, and in many other venues. She has her own greeting card line that she sells on her website. Blue Mountain Arts Greeting Card Company was very interested in Jean Marie's writings and tested them across the United States.

A recent article in Newsday about Jean Marie's cards said: "Her topics reach far beyond traditional greeting cards. She marks happy occasions such as the aforementioned adoption

> Jean Marie's mission is to make a difference in people's lives and share the truth that God exists, and Jesus loves us.

—'Only God knew that their hearts were going to melt at the first sight of your precious face'— or becoming a police officer —'It takes a very special person to want to protect complete strangers.'"

But many also deal with helping people through a struggle, for instance, to support those considering divorce, battling addiction, or dealing with a loved one's suicide. "These are topics you will not usually find in stores," Prince says.

Since then, many opportunities to speak about the book have been put before her. Even though Jean Marie has no college education or prior experience as a writer or songwriter, she feels confident that God showed her the way so that she could share her spiritual experiences, as well as God's love, with everyone.

Jean Marie's mission is to make a difference in people's lives through her book that shares the truth that God exists, and Jesus loves us. She is grateful for the many ways God has helped her and changed her circumstances positively, which is why she wants to share it with others. Her speaking engagements have inspired many and she is comforted to know that she is helping many hurting and desperate people. She would like to continue to do speaking engagements throughout the country; sharing God's love with others and spreading His good word to every person she meets.

God has blessed her with the ability to write these inspirations so it helps others through their own trials. Jean Marie has seen several relationships mended because of the inspirations in her book and is humbled that God chose her for this purpose.

Jean Marie is very grateful for her book and CD Albums. She has learned that with God, all things are possible! To generate awareness about her book, she has created YouTube videos so people can follow her along this *"Inspired Blessings"* journey. Her passion touches many people and is the impetus for her number one cause—*"to see everyone have eternal life in heaven."*

Jean Marie's purpose in life is to share with everyone that "For God so loved the world, that he gave his only begotten Son, that whosoever believeth in him should not perish, but have everlasting life." John 3:16

WORDS OF WISDOM

"My purpose is to see everyone in Heaven, where there is no more pain and no more sorrow. This is my passion, and the best gift from

God . . . one that I can share with everyone. I have had many different types of sales positions, but this is the most important job I have ever had. Offering the free gift of eternal life through Jesus is the most unique and wonderful gift that anyone could ever receive."

Keep "Inspired Blessings" within arm's reach, to help give you comfort when others are at a loss for words!"

Questions to Ponder

- *Do you have something that would bring comfort to others that you could share?*
- *What are some of the ways you can spread the word?*
- *What do you need to do to get started today?*

CONNECT WITH JEAN MARIE

jeanmarieprince.com

inspiredblessings@gmail.com

631-361-6926

Chapter Twenty-Five

AGAINST THE ODDS

Lhea Scotto

Take the first step in faith. You don't have to see the whole staircase, just take the first step. ~ Martin Luther King

*L*hea's life dramatically changed when she became a single mom of three boys all under five years old. Her parents moved to Florida within the first year of her divorce and she felt very alone . . . even abandoned. She went for therapy, where she explored her self-image, negative feelings, and lack of confidence in making the right choices for herself and family. She also made the decision to get a job, find someone to help her with her children, and raise her sons in the best way possible; this would give them every opportunity for her children and herself to have a great life.

She remembers people discouraging her from her dreams. One time, while visiting her doctor, she told him she needed to get someone to watch her children so that she could go back to work. His immediate response was that she would never find anyone to watch three little boys! Guess what, she did. Another time when she wanted to start dating, her dad said to her, "Who would want you with three little boys!" That turned out not true as well. She wanted to buy a house and her accountant said that she couldn't do that–her credit was not good enough. Yes, another success–she found someone that could do an unconventional loan. She persevered despite negativity and fear. Most importantly, her children grew up, went to college, graduated without loans and became successful and very fine young men! She is a very proud mom of these three young men, who are caring, loving adults who possess a great work ethic.

Life changed for Lhea again when she mentioned to her friend, Ellen, a forerunner in the business community and a mentor, that she wanted to get involved in volun-

> Through her willingness to look within, she felt powerful and kept on overcoming obstacles and meeting goals.

teer work. Ellen referred her to the March of Dimes, an organization that saved the lives of newborns and their moms who have medical issues after childbirth. Lhea became an active participant on their Women of Distinction Committee for about five years. They honored women who made a difference in their community and raised money by running a gala in their honor. The wonderful feeling she got from volunteering became a springboard to an active "volunteer" career.

Lhea focused on helping people and changing lives. When her children were still young, she joined Parents Without Partners. This was perfect for her as she was struggling with money issues and they offered activities for the kids with substantial discounts. She joined a committee and began writing a Member-of-the-Month column. Of course, she didn't know then that she was paving the way for a writing career. Funny how things work out!

She received so many gifts from volunteering: she believes the most important ones were leadership, development and teamwork. She thinks back to the Long Island Center for Business & Professional Women where she spent more than fourteen years of her life and how this happened. First, she joined a committee, and then she led several committees. After several years she became a board member, then Vice President. The organization's current president stepped down–then she stepped up to the plate and became President. Rather than complain, she saw an opportunity to change things and be part of something great. She was able to accomplish a turnaround with the support of a great board and team of volunteers. She is the proud recipient of the 'President's Achiever's Award' from the Long Island Center for Business & Professional Women, and for a citation received from Andrew Cuomo for leadership and volunteerism.

Another life-changing event in her life was her introduction to motivational tapes (not CDs, LOL). The first one she heard was the *"Psychology of Achievement"* by Brian Tracy. Brian taught about visualization–when you become clear on what you want, you can obtain it. She attributes visualization to starting her own business and buying the house she wanted. And years later she visualized through her own bubble concept the person she wanted to meet and who she would later marry. Through her willingness to look within and utilize the resources available in these motivational tapes, she felt powerful and kept on overcoming obstacles and meeting goals.

Every morning when she awakens, she likes to think of ways that she can contribute to the world. It could be helping a neighbor, making a donation, teaching her grandchild how to read or just helping someone at the grocery store who is being challenged.

What Lhea has learned is that, if you really care about people, it will overflow into all aspects of your life. When she does resumé writing for her clients, she cares about each one of them. She creates a document that expresses who they are and what makes them special. *She gets a real thrill when they call her or email her to let her know that they got several interviews . . . or even a job. She really believes that one person can change the world.*

WORDS OF WISDOM

Based on her experiences, she suggest that you surround yourself with people who encourage you, not discourage you—because when people say negative or fearful things, they are usually talking about themselves. Look at life as an adventure, see opportunities, come up with a plan, and take small steps. Feel good about little accomplishments. Be a mentor and motivator to others.

QUESTIONS TO PONDER

- *When faced with obstacles in your life, what resources did you use?*
- *Did anyone ever discourage you from fulfilling your dreams?*
- *In what ways can you contribute to the world today?*
- *What opportunities have you had to become a springboard for volunteering or mentoring?*
- *Is there someone on your gratitude list to thank for all their love and support?*

CONTACT LHEA

Lhea@822jobs.com

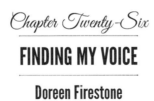

FINDING MY VOICE

Doreen Firestone

"Surrender, but never give up. Do whatever it takes to make yourself ready and able to do the work that God created you to do."

*D*oreen Firestone's mission in life is to lead people home to God through her art and by sharing her history. The singer/actress and playwright/composer of the famous musical, *The Prodigal Daughter*, turned her life full circle with the help of God's grace. But it didn't happen overnight.

An early childhood experience of family mental illness, abuse, and alcoholism found Doreen estranged from life and God. It was soon apparent that God intervened when she could not help herself. At the age of 20, she began the healing process from a childhood trauma that left scars inside her heart. She was able to put past wounds behind, and subsequently help others find their way. Through compassion and love for people and their struggles, she was strengthened with the courage to move past her fears and doubts. Through it all, she came away knowing that her greatest hope is to inspire many people to use their talents and experiences so they, too, would be willing and able to help others.

She discovered that she had many God-given talents, such as a gift for storytelling, an operatic voice which has been honed with the help of a voice teacher for the past 35 years, musical sensibilities, and an ear for hearing a melody within herself. It allowed her to transfer the melodies from her fingers to the piano, and finally, to the written page. Doreen wrote a story, a presentation about the prodigal's journey home to God, which mirrored her own spiritual journey. In *The Prodigal Daughter*, she discovered that her performance touched the hearts and minds of her audience profoundly. During one particular performance, she was so enthralled by the reaction of the audience that she knew the power of God's presence filled the entire room. It was an awe-inspiring experience she would never forget.

As she journeyed along with the twists and turns of life, her music, humorous stories, and deep insights gave her confidence, unlimited potential, and clarity on how to express her mission. Through self-acceptance, forgiveness, and gratitude she was ignited to write her next show. In her presentation, "Finding Your Voice," Doreen traces her autobiographical history and the discovery of her true self. In this work of releasing false beliefs, it has now become clear to her that her purpose is to guide others in their quest to find their voice in every situation.

> Through it all, she came away knowing that her greatest hope is to inspire many people to use their talents and experiences so they, too, would be willing and able to help others.

Doreen's truth poem

I don't mind

What's behind

It had to be

For me to find

My true mind

WORDS OF WISDOM

All experiences contribute to making a person wiser, and Doreen is no exception to this rule. She offers reassuring words to those who are floundering or have not yet found their way: "Never, ever use your past as an excuse. Surrender the past and its negative hold, and let other people in. It takes courage, it takes commitment, and it takes LOVE. Let go and let God love you!"

QUESTIONS TO PONDER

- *How has finding your voice helped you use your talents and gifts to follow your dream?*
- *Is there a dream you have that you've been putting off accomplishing? Name it.*
- *What's stopping you from pursuing your dream?*
- *If there is one thing you can do in the next week that would help you get closer to fulfilling your dream, and you have no fear of failure in the completion of this task, what would it be?*
- *Who in your life could you ask to support you in facing your*

fears and forging on ahead? Write down one or two names. And then... ask them!

CONNECT WITH DOREEN

Doreen@FirestoneProductionsUnlimited.com

www.FirestoneProductionsUnlimited.com

Chapter Twenty-Seven

THE NEXT STEPS ON YOUR JOURNEY

Teresa Velardi and Bill Reitzig

"Be committed to making a difference in the lives of others using your God-given gifts and talents with passion and purpose, and all of God's great universe will conspire in your favor."

*T*eresa has a heart for people and volunteerism; she often wonders where her attention will be drawn next. She believes all people can make a difference in the lives of others, particularly while using their God-given gifts and talents. She's volunteered at her church for years, from working with the children to leading a team of people who give their time to help others take their "Next Steps" on their spiritual journey. Over her lifetime, she has learned that everyone matters . . . Everyone!

When she left Long Island in 2002, Teresa made Pennsylvania her home, but her heart has never really left her hometown of Rocky Point, where she grew up with people who have become lifelong friends. Teresa entered Rocky Point Schools in the second grade, and many of those bright-eyed second graders are still in her life today, many years later with children and grandchildren of their own. One of the many things Teresa learned from her late mother, Freida, is how to be a friend. At her mom's funeral were people who were her mother's friends for more than fifty years!

Bill Reitzig and Teresa have been friends since the second grade. Though they don't see each other very often, their hearts, along with those of many of their class-mates, are connected for life. They are members of the first graduating class of Rocky Point High School with just over one hundred students graduating with great esteem from what was then, the new high school. Members of that class weren't just friends; they were and still are family. Many of those classmates know what it means to be and to have lifelong friends. Some have been lost along the way to various illnesses, accidents, and causes, yet none had experienced a loss as tragic as Bill and his wife Sandy did on April 22, 2016.

> Being aware and proactive in your home, your business, your social circles, and your community can save lives.

Bill and Sandy's beautiful family includes two daughters, Jenna and Lissette, and a son, Billy. To many people, it seemed they had not a care in the world. But, as we all know, things are not always what they seem. Their son, Billy, struggled with addiction to opioids. He was in and out of treatment, desiring to be free from the torture and torment of the daunting addiction.

Addiction doesn't discriminate. Anyone, even someone as loyal, loving, caring, respectful, polite, and sometimes tough, as Billy was, "particularly when it came to defending his friends," can become addicted to something. There are drugs of many kinds, not just "street drugs." Alcohol, prescription drugs, food, sex, shopping, or gambling can consume you. Nearly anything can become an addiction; if it's consuming your thoughts and taking control of your life, you can probably say it's an addiction. Addiction is a sickness that millions live with through a daily reprieve, trusting a higher power, as suggested by the many Twelve-Step Programs; others are not so fortunate to have that reprieve.

Billy fought his daily battle with the help of *Hope House Ministries, where they provide compassionate, comprehensive, and competent care for the poor, the marginal, and the wounded among us. This commitment is woven in the Gospel vision that all life is sacred, and every human person is unique and has the right to be respected and protected.* Their founder, Father Frank Pizzarelli, stated, "for the most part, Billy's life was good."

His family loved him through good days and challenging days. Then, on what his father, Bill, calls "a dark day," Billy decided to try heroin. Even in anticipation of a great weekend with family and friends ahead, and looking forward to it, Billy sold something he valued and bought heroin, for the first time, the ONLY time. It took his life and at the same time, freed his tortured soul.

For those of us who are parents, the loss of a child is our worst nightmare, yet this family, even amid the nightmare, has chosen to focus outward and bring hope, awareness, and support to others as they walk through the ongoing pain of such great, unimaginable loss.

Addiction is a cruel, life-debilitating, murderous disease that does not discriminate. We hear about people who were famous and lost their lives, many at young ages. In the music industry alone, many talented people fell victim to addiction, but until recently, the nation turned a blind eye to the magnitude of the problem. In the past, the focus was on street drugs, and no one was paying attention to the prescription medications people were getting hooked on.

Teresa knows, firsthand, having been married to an addict, what addiction to prescription drugs can do to an individual, a marriage, a family, and a community.

Through two events, each on the anniversary of Billy's passing, Bill and Sandy have focused on raising awareness, bringing people together whose lives have been greatly affected by the loss of a loved one to drug/alcohol addiction or are still struggling to break free from addiction. The first was *Hope Walk for Addiction* in 2017, and the second, *War on Addiction Rally*, took place in 2018. People from all over Long Island have come out in support of these events, many who have been affected by the opioid addiction crisis. *War on Addiction* was also represented at the Town of Brookhaven's 2019 Fourth of July event on Bald Hill, Farmingville. All funds from these events are donated to *Hope House Ministries* in Port Jefferson, NY.

Opioid addiction is the biggest drug crisis this country has ever seen and has taken the lives of over 400,000 people. A recent article in Newsday spoke of a study titled, *"The Staggering Cost of Long Island's Opioid Crisis."* The study revealed, "The opioid crisis is costing Long Island's economy roughly 8 billion a year in medical costs, lost worker productivity, and economic losses."

Bill and Dave Okorn, of the Long Island Community Foundation (LICF) have been lobbying The Long Island Association (LIA)to be proactive in addressing opioid and other addiction issues. Together, with the help of other Long Islanders, Bill continues the conversation to raise awareness from families to foundations, medical professionals, hospitals, gathering signatures and petitioning government officials. While big pharma and some rehab centers would rather sweep this crisis under the rug, some of the manufacturers are finally being held responsible by the courts to put some of the billions made from the sale of opioid drugs back into society to help clean up the mess they created.

They say time heals all wounds, but Teresa isn't so sure about that. Bill, Sandy, and their daughters continue to miss and grieve their unfathomable loss, yet have courageously stepped into the arena where Billy lost his battle. They continue to give hope to many others and have supported the ministry that supported their son. Bill has been invited to be a member of the board of Hope House in 2020 and is wholeheartedly committed to their mission.

WORDS OF WISDOM

Just because this deadly situation may not have touched your family or circle of friends doesn't mean that it won't. Being aware and proactive in your home, your business, your social circles, and your community can save lives. Bill and Sandy Reitzig are on a mission to make a difference in the lives of others.

QUESTIONS TO PONDER

- *Have you or your family been affected by addiction?*
- *If you were in Bill and Sandy shoes, having lost a child, or anyone dear to you, what would you do?*
- *Do you have the courage to step up and bring hope to those families and addicts still suffering?*

- *How can you make a difference?*

CONNECT WITH TERESA

Email: teresavelardi@gmail.com

Phone: 570-230-4185

Hope House Ministries

Website: www.hhm.org

To learn more, go to:

www.waronaddictionrally.com

FIRED UP SONG

Lyrics: Donna Cariello - Music: Michael Mancuso

Fired Up is officially registered with the United States
Copyright Office on 4/30/2013

Nicholas, 2003

Christopher, 2019

Together we can share.
We can get excited.
Together we can care and get that spark ignited.

With a little help from you there is nothing we can't do.
A gift of love, a gift of light like a fire burning bright.

Come on help each other out.
Show you care without a doubt.
The good you do comes right back to you.

Fired up to give & share.
Fired up to show you care.
Burning bright…
Fired up with love.
Fired up to strike a spark.
Fired up light up the dark.
Burning bright…
Fired up with Love

Together we can share.
Let's get our soul get excited.
Together we can care and get that spark ignited.

With a little help from you there is nothing we can't do.
A gift of love, a gift of light like a fire burning bright.

Come on help each other now.
We can make it work somehow.
The good you do impacts all of you.

Fired up to give & share.
Fired up to show you care.
Burning bright…
Fired up with love.
Fired up to strike a spark.
Fired up light up the dark.
Burning bright…
Fired up with Love

To Get Your FREE Digital Song Download of "Fired UP"
go to: www. TheLongIslandWay.com / Song

ABOUT THE AUTHOR

We each have ingredients that make up our lives. Here are the ingredients to the recipe of my life:

Being the baby of six children and growing up in the Jamaica Queen's projects within a very diverse community, my childhood felt like I was part of one big family having fun in a play-ground. I always remember being on the move, helping Mommy and my siblings with whatever was needed. I was the "go-getter" kid and still am; I love being a part of the action.

Spending most of my time playing ring-a-levio, Johnny on the Pony, handball, basketball, softball, and other outdoor games filled the excitement of daily living. Being part of a team and loving the game as a natural-born athlete became a huge part of who I am. I also have fond memories going Christmas caroling with my family and being in front of everyone else because of my "cute and contagious smile," not my voice (hahaha) because I can't hold a note. Mom and my siblings taught me that I could do anything I put my mind to. Nicknamed "peanut" and later on, "the energizer bunny" I was full of life like my Dad, who was likened to a thoroughbred racehorse. Unable to sit still in elementary school, I needed extra help with reading comprehension and my ability to focus on reading a book.

Why is it important for you to know this? This so-called defect of character evidenced at a young age became an asset. Through the grace of God's guidance, love, and support system in my life, that extra help has come full circle with the creation of the "*Ambassadors of HOPE*" book and "*Fired Up*" Song.

Coming from a big family with the sibling order of boy, girl, boy, girl, I always compared my family to that of the TV show, "The Brady Bunch." I could and still can always find the best in everyone and the positive solution for everything. Mom held the family together and my sister Diane lovingly embraced the role of mother's helper. She also excelled at being the voice of reason and became a role model at a very early age for our family and our community. I remember participating in Catholic Charity events at church where I met Timmy, an awesome counselor and church member. Diane would quiz me about Timmy who later became my brother-in-law. Both Timmy and Diane play a very active role in giving back to the community to this day.

I believe I am following in my mother's footsteps. Mom was very creative and business savvy. She started her own jewelry business with my cousin, Joyce. We would all hustle off to NYC to purchase goods and ultimately watch the beads be transformed into the most beautiful jewelry; then I would help pack up and travel to different locations on Long Island to showcase what she created. As you can see, I got my creative juices and entrepreneurial vision from my Mom, who was also my best friend.

After college, I worked at FedEx, where I was given the training and skills to perform at the highest level of my career. I received many accolades —*Manager of the Year, Community Service Celebrating Excellence Award, Development of the New Hire Process Awards,* and many other honors from various nonprofit organizations. The FedEx slogan, *"Absolutely—Positively—Overnight,"* personifies the attitude of always delivering the package no matter what the circumstances leading to my strong work ethic. FedEx instilled in me the ability to deliver the package, the message, the event, the book, and whatever else my personal and professional life requires.

As a person who loves helping people, FedEx gave me the platform and tools to reach out through United Way to the following local nonprofit organizations: Family and Children Association, March of Dimes, American Cancer Society, Long Island Cares, LIVE—Long Island Volunteer Enterprise, AHRC, as well as many others. I loved to round-up all the FedEx managers and leave the office to help those in need of food, planting, painting, building, funding, and more. One of my favorite events was the softball tournament to benefit Ronald McDonald House of Long Island, where we competed with one another in a teambuilding atmosphere for a cause we all believed in.

FedEx offered a buyout to all management, so I took this opportunity to start my life as an entrepreneur, or like my son, Nicholas, would say, "I was replanted to bloom where I am now." I was asked to be on the board of directors for "The Long Island Center for Business and Professional Women," where I made friends for life. My buddy, Lhea played an instrumental part in my career. She brought in Andrew Morrison as a speaker and expert on small business marketing and development, to give his Small Business Boot Camp presentation. It was soul-searching and it inspired me to do what would be my next career choice. He asked us to reflect on our life and work experience, and proposed the following questions about abilities, talents and path:

- What are you good at?

- What comes naturally to you?

- What do you love to do?

- What is your calling?

At that instant, I had a lightbulb moment! I love helping people, and I identified a mutual need in both the business and nonprofit community. Every business needs to be promoted, and every nonprofit needs great exposure and a large audience. They both require support with business clients and donors, and both need to be connected to these relationships. Thus, *The Long Island Way* was born: Where businesses and nonprofits grow together for mutual benefit based on the 'Spirit of Giving.'" Our logo is a finger painting posted on the cover of the book by my son Christopher when we played arts and crafts at our kitchen table. It was a masterpiece. We created a cause-marketing platform and my wonderful team lead by Susan McDonald and Marie Cantone helped engage hundreds of businesses and nonprofits in relationships, leading to raising over a million dollars. We've captured the hearts and minds of individuals and companies committed to collaboration and cooperation, which lead to our "Breakfast of Champions" celebration.

I am so grateful to have received recognition as a honoree from the Long Island Press and Beverly Fortune as a *Fortune 52 Extraordinary Women* for making a significant contribution to the nonprofit community. It was very rewarding to be honored for my work. This was a "Hallmark moment," for me because I felt like a "Rock Star" on stage with other amazing honorees. I feel humbled and very blessed to be recognized for the work I do with my abilities God has given me.

The greatest gifts are my two sons, Nicholas and Christopher. I am privileged, honored and eternally grateful to be their MOM. As Aunt Joanne says, "It takes a village to raise a child." That is so true, and they have helped me raise the bar to be a better person, daughter, sister, friend, and yes . . . a better mother. Thank you, God!

Every day, I passionately live and breathe this core belief, which is *to make the world a better place . . . one person, one organization, or one company at a time.* Every day, with my family, friends and strangers . . . I walk the talk. I look for the best in people and do my best to change attitudes, to uncover choices, to contribute welcoming ideas, and to spark enthusiasm . . . one person and one day at a time!

> *We Rise By Lifting Others.*
> *~Robert Gree Ingersoll*

Made in the USA
Middletown, DE
07 November 2019